# RICHER LIFE

# How the Generosity Mindset Transforms You and Changes the World

## René Schlaepfer

Visual Design: Amy Buller & Kéla Toback

Printed locally with vegetable-based inks on recycled paper
at Community Printers, Santa Cruz, California, USA

Want to see sermons, small group videos,
and more related to this book?
**tlc.org/richerlife**

# Contents

# Read This First

**W**ould you like a richer life? A life filled with more joy, more confidence, a greater sense of meaning and purpose?

I was in the San Jose airport bookstore recently, desperately seeking a book for the long trip ahead, when I noticed a magazine I'd never before considered in-flight reading material: The Harvard Business Review. I flipped it open to the cover story, by Harvard professor and best-selling author Clayton M. Christensen. His first paragraph had me hooked.

Christensen says he'd grown tired of seeing so many Harvard grads return to school for visits as unhappy, lonely, unfulfilled people––though they'd often achieved phenomenal success in business. So he now takes the final lecture in his class each semester to basically tell his students, "Congratulations on completing your Harvard education. Nothing you have learned here will make you happy."

Realizing his students will be skeptical, he quotes research showing the most satisfying long-term motivator in life actually isn't making money; it's being generous. In the end, he says, "We will measure our lives by our contribution, not our accumulation." Counter-intuitively, generosity makes us feel richer, more satisfied. As Jesus observed: "It is more blessed to give than to receive."

Research proves it: The May/July 2012 edition of the journal Psychological Science summarized several studies indicating people are much happier when generous. Another study even showed lower inflammation levels in generous people. Generous people tend to live healthier, longer lives. But there's a caveat: Researchers Netta Weinstein and Richard Ryan found that people who kept a daily diary felt better on the days they did something to help a person or a cause, but only if it was their choice. When they felt pressured, those positive effects almost disappeared.

In other words, to be fulfilling, generosity must be motivated internally, by joy and delight, not by guilt or obligation. That's why, when you read about generosity in the Bible, it always starts with God's generosity toward you. The big idea: I am the recipient of God's lavish grace every day. When my imagination is captured by that, my generosity will develop naturally and joyfully. Generosity must be my *identity* before it becomes my *activity*.

That's the object of this daily devotional: To help you increasingly recognize the generosity of God toward you, so your sense of blessing keeps overflowing to others.

To be honest, most teaching I've heard in churches on generosity leaves me cold precisely because it misses the mark in this respect. It doesn't start with grace. It's all about guilt. That's why I feel so blessed to be exploring this in the context of the place I serve as pastor, Twin Lakes Church in Aptos, California. TLC has to be one of the most generous churches on the planet. I think it's because people there are grounded in a sense of God's grace, which spills out in many amazing ways.

That Harvard Business Review article had me so riveted I nearly missed my plane! I quickly bought it and rushed for my gate, and on that flight I began a journey of research resulting in the book you're now reading. I'll be revealing in these pages some of the studies and the Scriptures that meant the most to me. This little devotional is designed to be read daily, Monday through Saturday, for seven weeks. It's part of a comprehensive study of generosity originating at Twin Lakes Church. You can also watch sermons and discussion-starter videos, all for free, at tlc.org/richerlife.

Let's enjoy reveling in God's lavish grace—and reflecting it—together!

# WEEK 1

# Our Generous God

---

🕊 OUR GENEROSITY IS THE REFLECTION
OF WHAT WE HAVE PERSONALLY
COME TO KNOW ABOUT JESUS.
- LOUIE GIGLIO

---

# The Grace of Giving

**But since you excel in everything—in faith, in speech, in knowledge, in complete earnestness and in the love we have kindled in you—see that you also excel in this grace of giving. 2 Corinthians 8:7 (NIV)**

In today's verse Paul defines giving as a "grace", a character trait that reflects God's heart, just like faith or love. As we begin this study it's important to explore this biblical understanding of generosity. In Scripture, generosity is not just (or even mostly) associated with giving money. It's a *quality*, one of the personality traits of God we reflect as we become more like Christ.

TED Talk speaker Dr. John Thornton is an expert on money. He teaches Accounting Ethics and in 2017 released his ironically titled book *Jesus' Terrible Financial Advice*. In a true God-moment, I happened to run into John when working on this devotional. I asked if we could meet over breakfast, and although he was on vacation, he agreed. I took advantage of the serendipitous opportunity and quizzed him about an exercise he details in his book.

John compiled a list of all 1,300 verses in the Bible on money, and then studied and categorized each one. He expected the vast majority to be about our obligation to give money away. But he was completely surprised by what he found.

The top category was not about our need to be generous; *it was about God's generosity to us!* Verse after verse spoke of God providing us with both spiritual and material blessings. The next largest category? Our need to give? Nope. Verses warning about the deceitfulness of wealth. "Money makes a good servant but a terrible master," as John says.

*Verses about giving to others came in a distant third.* Seems God wants us to live in the daily reality of his gifts to us, and to be warned about making money a false god, before we move on to generosity. It's like our giving will somehow be tainted with reluctance or pride if we don't really get those first two points down.

That's why we'll kick off every week in this devotional book with a meditation on God's generosity toward us. Our giving is a reflexive response to the grace of God in our lives. True generosity doesn't just come out of altruism or philanthropy—it comes out of *joy*.

Someone has called this "whole-life generosity": Appreciating the abundance of God toward you, and letting that overflow in every way and in every direction. *Whole-life generosity starts with having your imagination captured by a vision of the rich blessings God pours out on you.*

I want to repeat this point because it's so important: The Bible never initiates its discussions of generosity with a parental scolding to "share". It always begins with enthralling descriptions of God's lavish generosity toward us! *We* give because *He* first gave to us. Our giving is the *reaction* to the initial *action*: God's amazing grace.

*Grace.* That's another word for "undeserved, lavish, outrageous generosity". It's the air you and I breathe as Christians. Let's rediscover it—and radiate it— together!

"We're most like God when we're giving."– Dixie Fraley

*Gracious Heavenly Father, help me to revel in your generosity toward me and reflect it joyfully to others! Please bless all who are joining in this study. May their lives be enriched in every way!*

# Through the Eyes of a Child

**Jesus said, "Mark this: Unless you accept God's kingdom in the simplicity of a child, you'll never get in." Luke 18:17 (TM)**

I enjoy being with our one-year-old grandson Freddy so much. One reason: He's amazed by absolutely everything! Stuff I take completely for granted is the source of utter fascination for him. I love watching how Freddy opens and closes cabinet doors, over and over, amazed each time; how gently he brushes his fingers across velvety rose petals; how engrossed he is in the buttons of an old TV remote, even if they don't do a thing.

I suspect that sense of wonder is one of the characteristics Jesus loved in little children. They're not calloused to God's gifts all around them. When our daughter was very little she prayed with passion at the dinner table, "Dear Lord, thank you SO MUCH for this food, and also thank you SO MUCH for elephants. And for sand. Amen." When's the last time you thanked God for elephants? Or sand? Probably never. But don't you think they're pretty cool?

As you walk through this week, look for things to thank God for, things you may not have ever thanked him for before, things that delight you. Write down a small list of blessings you notice on the next page. We'll look at them again later.

One more thing about little kids: They still respond with joy to the simple lyrics, "Jesus loves me, this I know." In Luke 18, Jesus makes today's comments about little children right after his story about the two men who went to the temple to pray. The first man boasts of his own righteousness. The second man humbly prays, "God, have mercy on me, a sinner." It's that admission of my powerlessness in the face of my own weakness that is also part of the simple, child-like faith Jesus values. Thank God for his blessings of grace with child-like wonder today.

*Lord, thank you for the wonders all around me. Help me see them with the eyes of a child!*

# GENEROSITY PROJECT
# Gratitude Journal

Begin a habit of noticing God's generosity to you! Throughout this study, contribute to this list of small and large blessings you notice around you, things that delight you that perhaps you've never realized you're grateful for. How to begin? Note the things that make you smile (for example, while writing just now I realized I was super-thankful for roller wheels on luggage, for friends who share their home-grown tomatoes, and for the new remix of Sgt. Pepper. But had I *thanked* God for any of that? Not until now).

_____

_____

_____

_____

_____

_____

_____

_____

_____

_____

(continued on back pages of book)

# The Prodigal Father

**The father called to the servants, 'Quick! Bring a clean set of clothes and dress him. Put the family ring on his finger and sandals on his feet. Then get a grain-fed heifer and roast it. We're going to feast! We're going to have a wonderful time! My son is here—given up for dead and now alive! Given up for lost and now found!' Luke 15:22-24 (TM)**

Today's verses come from the familiar parable in Luke 15, often called "the prodigal son". But really the prodigal in this story is the father. "Prodigal" means "giving something on a lavish scale; spending money freely." The father lavishes this extravagant feast on his completely undeserving rascal of a son—and Jesus is saying, that's what God is like!

Max Lucado writes, "God's greatest creation is not the flung stars or the gorged canyons, it's his eternal plan to reach his children. Behind his pursuit of us is the same brilliance behind the rotating seasons and the orbiting planets. Heaven and earth knows no greater passion than God's personal passion for you and your relationship with him."

There's a very important spiritual principle here: You are significant not because of *what you do*, but because of *who you are*, the beloved child of God. A richer life—the richest life possible—grounds personal significance not in *changing activity*, but in *unchanging identity*. Your generosity toward others will be infinitely more joyful and fulfilling (and sustainable) when you realize your generosity is not what makes you significant; it's a reflection of your joy in your infinite significance to God!

Jedd Medefind wrote a recent article in Christianity Today about the severe burnout he sees in many people devoted to social justice. The most public example: The founder of *Invisible Children*, Jason Russell. He went into a tailspin in late 2014 after his organization, devoted to freeing the child soldiers of Ugandan warlord Joseph Kony, became the hottest social justice organization on earth. Now Russell says what led to his burnout was "listening to the ego more than the Spirit." He says he made no provision for "how to navigate achieving inner spiritual peace and tranquility."

The life of generosity cannot be sustained apart from a deep inner life. "If you abide in me . . . you will bear much fruit," Jesus promised (John 15:5). Abiding is not laboring. Abiding is all adoration and wonder and undeserved grace. Medefind observes, "Any other source of nourishment—whether pure-hearted idealism, desire for recognition, or sincere ache at others' pain—may propel us for a time. Eventually, though, the world's great hurt will outlast our passion to address it. If we have no source beneath the surface, we will eventually run dry."

This is the problem with the embittered second son in Jesus' parable. He tells his father, "All these years I have *slaved* for you and you never gave me a thing..." His heartbroken father corrects him, "My son, all I have is yours..." That son labored only with his never-ending tasks in sight, never appreciating his father's generosity which surrounded him every day!

So dig deep into this truth, sons and daughters of God: Your Father longs for you, loves you, lavishes his riches on you. Like the sons in this parable, you can't earn his love. You don't deserve it. You simply receive it. And it surrounds you all the time! As you go through your day today, meditate on the idea that the same creator who made all the wonders around you, from trees to birds to sea, *loves you!*

*Lord, thank you for your lavish, prodigal love!*

# You Are Wanted

**How we praise God, the Father of our Lord Jesus Christ, who has blessed us with every blessing in heaven because we belong to Christ. Long ago, even before he made the world, God chose us to be his very own through what Christ would do for us; he decided then to make us holy in his eyes, without a single fault—we who stand before him covered with his love. His unchanging plan has always been to adopt us into his own family by sending Jesus Christ to die for us. And he did this because he wanted to! Ephesians 1:3-5 (TLB)**

Remember the elementary school awkwardness of standing in a group while two team captains chose their teams? The jocks got selected first. Then the popular kids. Then the funny kids. Then the friends of those kids. Meanwhile the rest of us (and yes, I was usually in this last bunch) concentrated on the pebbles at our feet and pretended not to care that two cool kids were arguing over who *had* to take us.

It's easy to imagine God looks at us the same way. He really started this world and then the whole salvation thing so the Michelangelos and Mother Teresas of this world could get on his team. You and me? We're just bench-warmers he *has* to accept, not the star players he really wants.

But look again at today's Scripture. You have been *chosen*. Long ago. Before God even made the world. That means before you could do anything to deserve it. Before you did anything right. Before you did anything wrong. He *chose you*. He chose you to be alive. He chose to reach you with his love. "And he did this because he *wanted* to!"

He didn't stop there. He blesses you "with every blessing in heaven." There is nothing you do to earn all this. You just receive it. Open your eyes and your heart to God's lavish, extravagant, generous blessings poured on you... now and forever!

*Thank you, God, for your grace to me! Thank you that you chose me!*

# Thirst Quenched

**As she stood behind him at his feet weeping, she began to wet his feet with her tears. Then she wiped them with her hair, kissed them and poured perfume on them. Luke 7:38 (NIV)**

In this story from Luke 7, a woman with a "sinful reputation" weeps with joy as she wipes Jesus' feet and perfumes them, thus scandalizing Simon, the hyper-religious Pharisee who had invited Jesus to dinner. She weeps in gratitude for the picture of a forgiving, gracious God that Jesus has been painting for "sinners" like her—people rejected by the religious establishment of her time.

Max Lucado draws a great picture: "What one discovery has she made that Simon hasn't? What one treasure does she cherish that Simon doesn't? Simple. God's love. We don't know when she received it. We aren't told how she heard about it. But we know this: She came thirsty. Thirsty from guilt. Thirsty from regret. Thirsty from countless nights of making love and finding none. She came thirsty. And when Jesus hands her the goblet of grace, she drinks. She doesn't just taste or sip it. She lifts the liquid to her lips and drinks, gulping and swallowing like the parched pilgrim she is. She drinks until the mercy flows down her chin and onto her neck and chest. She drinks until every inch of her soul is moist and soft. She comes thirsty and she drinks. She drinks deeply. Simon, on the other hand, doesn't even *know* he is thirsty."

Do you only *analyze* Christian doctrines like grace? Or do you drink deeply, moved to tears, rejoicing in worship because of God's lavish love?

Here's how this relates to generosity: Religious people (like me) frequently get stuck in the illusion that our "goodness" merits favor from God, and so makes us better than others. Our own moral behavior makes us proud, which is ironic because pride is the source of so much evil. In contrast, when we do good deeds out of a grateful response to God's lavish grace, then those deeds flow purely from love and not just from a sense of religious duty or need to do penance. *Gratitude is a much more sustainable motive than guilt or obligation!*

Today as you think of God's forgiveness of you in Christ, let your emotions go. Wash his feet with your tears. Thank him for quenching your thirst!

*Father, I bring nothing to you but my need. Thank you for quenching my thirst with your love and mercy.*

# Songs of Thanks

**I will praise God's name in song and glorify him with thanksgiving. Psalm 69:30 (NIV)**

I think people assume pastors like me are far more spiritual than we really are. Someone told me they'd been right next to my car in a traffic jam and tried to get my attention, but I was apparently so caught up in singing with a song on my car stereo that I didn't even notice them. "Pastor", they said, "that must have been one powerful time of worship for you, because you were clearly moved!" Indeed, I had been very emotional while bellowing a tune at the top of my lungs. I couldn't bring myself to tell them I'd been doing my best carpool karaoke to "More Than a Feeling" by Boston.

Maybe music moves you, as it does me. You listen to it and can't help but sing along. Today, and throughout this study, I encourage you to spend some of that time *worshiping in song*. Thanksgiving and music are mentioned together over and over in Scripture. There's something about that combination that brings us to our knees in wonder.

Perhaps the idea of singing praises to God is foreign to you, or maybe you don't know any songs of praise. There's a rich tradition of poetry and hymns that express thanksgiving. Try singing or reciting simple verses like these (And I hope you'll experience even more passion than I felt when I sang about "Maryann walking awaaaay...")

*Great is Thy faithfulness, O God my Father;*
*There is no shadow of turning with Thee;*
*Thou changest not, Thy compassions, they fail not;*
*As Thou hast been, Thou forever will be.*
*Great is Thy faithfulness!*
*Great is Thy faithfulness!*
*Morning by morning new mercies I see.*
*All I have needed Thy hand hath provided;*
*Great is Thy faithfulness, Lord, unto me!*

# GENEROSITY PROJECTS
# Get Involved

Find large and small ways to show your generosity during this study. It could be a simple act of kindness to a stranger. It might be a project with friends for someone elderly or needy.

Some ideas adapted from Jennifer Iacovelli's book *Simple Giving*:

- Hold a door open for a busy mom or elderly person
- Pick up trash in your neighborhood
- Bring doughnuts or other goodies to the local fire department or police station
- Check up on an elderly neighbor
- Allow a busy parent with kids to cut in front of you at the checkout line
- Offer free babysitting to a couple or single parent who could use a break
- Smile at strangers
- Write thank-you notes
- Join a community service project through your church (At TLC, we join other local churches on an outreach weekend each fall. There are projects for every age and skill level).
- Project Pajamas (See below)

Since 2007, judge Ari Symons and her team have led Project Pajamas in Santa Cruz County, collecting pajamas for the hundreds of local children and youth who are the oft-forgotten members of homeless families—or who lose their homes suddenly because of domestic violence or other sad situations. Many times these children have only the clothes on their backs. As Ari puts it, the gift of comfortable pajamas is a very tangible way to express, "there are people who know of your plight—and who care."

Over the past decade, 7,692 pajamas have been collected. Ari and her team have set a tenth-anniversary goal to reach the 10,000-pajama mark! If you're reading this book in 2017, consider donating one or more pair of pajamas by the end of this month to help attain this goal. There will be collection bins at Twin Lakes Church.

# WEEK 2
# Cultivating Gratitude

---

LET GRATITUDE BE THE PILLOW

UPON WHICH YOU KNEEL TO SAY

YOUR NIGHTLY PRAYER.

- MAYA ANGELOU

---

MONDAY
# Forget Not His Benefits

**Praise the Lord, my soul, and forget not all his benefits.
Psalm 103:2 (NIV)**

The wonders of creation around you.

The life-giving energy of the sun.

The people in your life.

The opportunities for work and service.

The church where you fellowship.

The very breath that sustains you.

The salvation that restores you.

And everything in between.

Today thank God for his benefits! Last week I suggested you write a small list of blessings you notice around you. Take a look at that list right now. Add some more items you've noticed that are God's gifts to you. And thank God for his generosity!

It's been said that life is God's gift to us. How we live our lives is our gift back to God.

*Lord, help me always stay grateful. And help me to reflect your generous spirit to others.*

# The Power of Gratitude

**Do not be anxious about anything, but in every situation, by prayer and petition, with thanksgiving, present your requests to God. And the peace of God, which transcends all understanding, will guard your hearts and your minds in Christ Jesus. Philippians 4:6,7 (NIV)**

No one wants to be a worrier. In today's verses, the Apostle Paul offers a substitute for the worry habit: Pray instead. And not just any kind of prayer... prayer that includes *thanksgiving*.

In 2007, UC Davis psychologist Robert Emmons began researching gratitude. He found that expressing gratitude improves mental, physical and relational well-being. And these effects tend to be long-lasting. He calls the habit of gratitude "emotional prosperity". Dr. Emmons says that in giving thanks, you are actually creating new neural pathways in your brain that replace your anxious or obsessive thought habits.

Another study published in the *Journal of Research in Personality* indicated that gratitude has been shown to decrease suicidal thoughts, independent of other depression symptoms.

So today take a few minutes to ask, "What am I grateful for?" Expand on that thought. Savor that blessing. Express thanks to God. Add it to the gratitude journal page from last week.

What are you thankful for today?

*Lord, I present to you these requests:* _____

_____

*And I also thank you for these blessings:* _____

_____

# Thanks in All Circumstances

**Give thanks in all circumstances; for this is God's will for you in Christ Jesus. 1 Thessalonians 5:18 (NIV)**

For seven years I watched my mother struggle with Alzheimer's disease. For much of her final two years she lived with us, giving our family a close-up view of her slow-motion death. I watched daily as all her abilities slipped slowly away, until even eating or speaking were nearly impossible. I'll admit I was bitter: Why should this beautiful woman, who had already had such a tough life, now experience this catastrophic illness?

Then I began contemplating the few words she could still say. At the end just three simple phrases were left in her vocabulary: "I love you." "Thank you." And often she would point to clouds or flowers and whisper, "Beautiful..."

"I love you." "Thank you." "Beautiful."

If she could do that, I thought, so could I. Why not try to infuse my own inner dialogue with her three-phrase vocabulary?

I began, inconsistently I'll admit, to practice noticing beautiful things. On my Instagram account I tried to make my daily "beauty hunt" a habit by publicly stating my intent to post a photo of one beautiful thing each day. You know what happened? I discovered that when I looked for beauty, I inevitably found it. My problem became not where to find a beautiful picture to post each day; it was deciding which photo to post! When I hit "send" on my daily post, I whispered a prayer to God: "Beautiful! Thank you. I love you." And Mom and I had some great three-phrase conversations.

You know what else I found? Appreciating beauty and giving thanks for life's treasures is not living in denial of life's suffering and challenges. It's what helps us cope with life's suffering and challenges.

Research shows that practicing the habit of gratitude consistently for just two weeks has positive effects lasting up to *six months*! It's how God made us. *Gratitude is the fuel we run on.*

So... what are you grateful for today?

"I don't have to chase extraordinary moments to find happiness—it's right in front of me if I'm paying attention and practicing gratitude." –Brene Brown

*Throughout the day, pray this simple prayer:*

*Beautiful. Thank you. I love you.*

# What Would it Take to Make You Feel Rich?

**Godliness with contentment is great gain. For we brought nothing into the world, and we can take nothing out of the world. 1 Timothy 6:6,7 (NIV)**

*Money* magazine asked its readers how much it would take to make them feel rich. According to the average *Money* reader, they'd need $5 million in liquid assets to feel truly wealthy.

So what would it take to make *you* feel rich?

Sir John Marks Templeton is a multi-billionaire and the founder of Templeton Mutual Funds. When asked the question, "What does it mean to be rich?", he replied with a one-word answer: *Gratitude*. He explained a phenomenon he had seen in his clients and friends over and over again: If someone has five dollars to their name and is thankful for that five dollars, then they are experiencing more satisfaction than someone with five million who just wants five million more. In his book *Discovering the Laws of Life*, Templeton talks about the importance of developing a spirit of thanksgiving. He says each moment holds something for which we can be thankful: Good health. A sunny day. Dry clothes. Friends. Libraries. Pets.

For most of us, our problem isn't that we're not rich. It's that we don't *feel* rich. The greatest way to increase your sensation of abundance is to learn to be grateful.

"Happiness cannot be traveled to, owned, earned, worn or consumed. Happiness is the spiritual experience of living every minute with love, grace, and gratitude." –Denis Waitley

*Father, help my enthusiasm and ambition to be grounded in deep appreciation and contentment!*

FRIDAY
# Remember to Say Thank You

**One of the ten lepers, when he saw he was healed, came back, praising God in a loud voice. He threw himself at Jesus' feet and thanked him—and he was a Samaritan. Jesus asked, "Were not all ten cleansed? Where are the other nine?" Luke 17:15-17 (NIV)**

In this story Jesus heals ten lepers of their disfiguring, fatal disease. Yet only one, a Samaritan (a religious and racial minority despised in Jesus' culture), comes back to say, "Thank you, Jesus!"

It's a sad but common human trait: We beg God for answers to prayer, and then when he blesses us, we often don't even say thanks. And most of the time we forget his answer before the year is over. The detail that this man was a Samaritan is consistent with an observation all the gospel writers made throughout Christ's ministry: It was the outsiders, the not-particularly-religious, who had a greater appreciation of what Jesus was all about than the religious people. Isn't it often the same now?

Today, don't be one of the nine. Be like the tenth guy, the one who took the time to give thanks.

As you go through your day today, make a mental list of prayers God has answered... crises he has seen you through... blessings he has given you... opportunities you have received... spiritual blessings you have in Christ. And each time you think of one... say thanks.

*Lord, here are some crises you have seen me through....*
*Here are some blessings you have given me....*
*Here are opportunities I have received...*
*For each, I am so grateful!*

# The Riches of the Cross

**He himself bore our sins in his body on the cross, so that we might die to sins and live for righteousness; "by his wounds you have been healed." 1 Peter 2:24 (NIV)**

Ever consider how bizarre it is that the cross would become the symbol of the Christian faith? We wear it as jewelry now—but think about what it really is. The cross was already a universal symbol in the Roman Empire that Jesus was born into. Everyone knew what it stood for.

Just before the time of Jesus, there was a slave revolt led by a man named Spartacus. The revolt was eventually put down and 6,000 rebel slaves were crucified. Their crosses lined the Appian Way, the road that led south out of Rome, for a distance of 130 miles. *One hundred and thirty miles of crosses.* Yes, the cross meant something to everyone in the Roman world: You mess with Rome, this will be your fate. It was a chilling symbol of imperial power.

But something strange happened to that symbol. In the mid-first century Roman Empire, suddenly people emerged who didn't fear the cross. They *loved* the cross. They put it in their art. They wrote songs about it. They thought the cross was so beautiful they put it on the graves of their loved ones. What in the world could have changed the meaning of the cross for them so completely, almost overnight?

These people said they had seen their teacher die on a Roman cross. And then three days later he was alive again. With a message: This is what is coming. A wave of life from God. To all who believe. Death and Roman power are not the end. Renewed *life* and *God's* power are the end. And the beginning.

Think of the riches of the cross: If you suffer from guilt or shame, there is *healing* in the cross of Christ because those sins are forgiven.

If you are going through tragedy or suffering, there is *comfort* in the cross, because you know Jesus gets it. He too suffered.

If you read headlines about this violent world and feel fear growing inside you, there is *hope* in the cross—because God took this symbol of hopelessness and political violence and flipped it on its head, showing how even when the worst happens, He will bring life. As Dr. Martin Luther King Jr. said, "It looked dark centuries ago... But thank God the crucifixion was not the last act. The resurrection affirms that what stops us does not stop God... death is not the end... life is not doomed to frustration and futility but can end up in fulfillment in the life and the resurrection of our Lord and Savior Jesus Christ."

As you meditate on the richness of God toward you, the cross is quite literally the *crux* of it all!

*Lord, thank you for the cross! Thank you for the depths of its meaning and beauty.*

# WEEK 3

# Generous Relationships

KINDNESS IS THE LANGUAGE WHICH

THE DEAF CAN HEAR AND THE BLIND

CAN SEE. - MARK TWAIN

# The Power of Awe

**For the Lord Most High is awesome! Psalm 47:2a (NIV)**

In a recent presentation at UC Berkeley, noted psychology professor Lani Shiota talked about what she calls "the science of awe". She points out how the sensation of awe actually transforms our bodies and minds in ways that are scientifically measurable.

Until she began her studies, there was little academic research on awe. Yet she discovered that a sense of awe is transformative, and perhaps even fundamental to human wellness. In her lab she found that awe is particularly powerful as a tool to subdue worry. She notes that, if we don't let ourselves experience awe, we become obsessed on minute details right in front of our noses. We forget the big picture. We become focused on our own worries and challenges. Or we think of ourselves as bigger, more important than we really are!

So step back and meditate in awe today on God—and on God's creation. Find some time to look at something that is bigger than you. The sky. The sea. The sun. A tree. Imagine the complex detail in that object.

Now, consider that the God who made all that... loves you! That is *truly* awesome!

Developing a growing appreciation of the spectacular generosity of God toward you is the essential first step to developing a truly generous heart.

*Lord, you are awesome!*

# Generosity in Relationships

**Be kind and compassionate to one another, forgiving each other, just as in Christ God forgave you. Ephesians 4:32 (NIV)**

Often overlooked, being generous is crucial to relationships. In fact, it's one of the top three indicators of a happy marriage, along with sexual satisfaction and commitment. According to a study by the University of Virginia's National Marriage Project, couples who reported a high amount of generosity in their relationship were *five times* more likely to say their marriage was "very happy."

So here are some ways to be generous in relationships today. Whether you practice these in a marriage relationship, or another relationship, try some of these ways to be relationally generous:

- Give someone a sincere compliment.
- Bring someone coffee or lunch.
- Write a kind note.
- Make a mental list of things you like about someone, and tell them.
- When you see a chore that needs to be done, do it.

Most important: Forgive. Forgiveness is the oil that helps relationships run smoothly. After all, it's the foundation of God's generosity toward you!

"Beginning today, treat everyone you meet as if they were going to be dead by midnight. Extend to them all the care, kindness and understanding you can muster, and do it with no thought of any reward. Your life will never be the same again."–Og Mandino

*Father, help me to be generous in my relationships this week. May I begin patterns of generosity that strengthen and grow my relationships for years to come.*

# Let it Go

**"Even if they sin against you seven times in a day and seven times come back to you saying 'I repent,' you must forgive them." Luke 17:4 (NIV)**

The ubiquitous soundtrack to the Disney hit "Frozen" has a song every little girl in America knows: *"Let It Go"*. That could also be the title of many passages of Scripture. But in the Bible, "let it go" usually has a different meaning. When people offend you, sin against you, hurt your feelings... *let it go*.

The religious leaders of Jesus' day taught you were to forgive someone three times for an offense, but not four. Jesus ups the ante considerably when he says to forgive those who offend you "seven times... in a day." Of course this doesn't mean you must trust someone who is untrustworthy. It means you let go of your anger. You let go of your resentment. You let go of your passion for vengeance. It's part of being relationally generous. *You* are generous with forgiving others... because God is generous in his forgiveness of *you*!

Jesus modeled this to the *nth* degree, of course, on the cross. He was betrayed, mocked, spit upon, beaten, and crucified. And he used one of his last breaths to say, "Father, forgive them, for they know not what they do." (Luke 23:34).

So today, when that driver cuts you off, when that person says something unkind, when that guy ahead of you in the express lane has 16 items in his cart...let it go.

"Kindness is in our power, even when fondness is not."
–Samuel Johnson

*Father, here are some things I am having a hard time letting go of...Please help me to be generous with forgiveness toward others, just as you are to me.*

# Kindness is the Glue

**I will tell of the kindnesses of the Lord, the deeds for which he is to be praised, according to all the Lord has done for us—yes, the many good things he has done for Israel, according to his compassion and many kindnesses.** Isaiah 63:7 (NIV)

In his book "The Science of Happily Ever After", psychologist Ty Tashiro summarizes decades of research on marriage. In all these studies, it seems happiness in relationships is really quite simple to predict. It comes down to... *kindness.* He says kindness is the single most important predictor of satisfaction and stability in a marriage. Kindness glues couples together.

In other studies of newlywed couples by renowned marriage researcher John Gottman, 87% of those who were kind to one another as newlyweds were still married years later. The majority of those who had been rude to one another when first married were divorced.

So look for ways to be kind to friends and family today. And not just grudgingly kind. Be lavishly generous with your kindness. Be kind to loved ones, co-workers, and even strangers you meet in stores or restaurants or on phone calls. Watch what happens!

And always remember how your kindness to others should reflect the lavish kindness God shows you!

"Through kindness a king's throne is made secure." – Solomon

*Lord, help me to be kind to everyone I meet today. Help my kindness to reflect your spectacular kindness to me.*

# Couriers of Wonder

**Every time we think of you, we thank God for you.**
**1 Thessalonians 1:2 (TM)**

We've been focusing this week on generosity in relationships. Are you generous with your gratitude to others?

In a TED Talk on happiness, Dr. Martin Seligman describes an assignment that almost universally creates a sense of deep happiness in research subjects: *Think of someone who has done something for you, write them a thank-you note... and then read it to them.*

Margaret Feinberg writes: "People are often the couriers of God's wonder in our lives. Take time to look around. Make a list of the people who have made a difference in your life. Express your gratitude to three of them. Pick up the phone. Send an email. Hand-write a personal note. Whatever form of expression you choose, know that as you express your appreciation, you'll be encouraging them to continue serving and helping others. Sit back and watch the wonder of gratitude unfold as you love those who mean the most to you."

Today is a day to say thanks! Write that note. Make that call. Write a blog or social media post about someone who has made a difference in your life!

*Thank you, God, for these "couriers of wonder" in my life, these people who are a blessing and delight:*

# SATURDAY
# Do You Get
# What You Give?

**(Jesus said) "Give, and it will be given to you. A good measure, pressed down, shaken together and running over, will be poured into your lap. For with the measure you use, it will be measured to you." Luke 6:38 (NIV)**

I love today's verse. But as pastor and author Robert Morris points out, it's one of the most frequently misapplied verses in the Bible. For one thing, most people assume Jesus is talking about giving money.

Back up a couple verses and look at the two verses right before this: "Be merciful, just as your Father is merciful. Do not judge, and you will not be judged. Do not condemn, and you will not be condemned. Forgive, and you will be forgiven." (Luke 6:36,37). It's in the very next sentence that Jesus says, "Give and it will be given to you." So in context it's clear he's applying this principle to *relationships*: Forgiveness and mercy and judgment and condemnation. He's pointing out that, generally speaking, whatever you give is going to come back to you. In spades. "A good measure, pressed down, shaken together and running over, poured into your lap."

It's sobering. If you give judgment, judgment will be given back to you. In fact, you'll get an overwhelming harvest of judgment! But if you give love, you'll get an abundant harvest of that. Of course, the principle also applies to generosity. Research shows generous people are attractive people. They are usually loved and treasured as friends.

Another misapplication of this Scripture: It's often used to present monetary gain as the primary motive for giving. "Give to God, and you'll get back! Isn't that a great deal?!" I've heard televangelists use this verse to try and manipulate people to send money to their ministries. But as Robert Morris puts it, "Do you really think that's what Jesus hopes we'll get out of this verse? Do you think he ever thought, 'Boy, if only my disciples would catch the vision of how to magically get more stuff'?" Jesus doesn't want us to catch the vision of *getting*. He wants us to catch the vision of *giving*.

Yes, there are benefits to giving. Researchers have shown that joyful altruism lowers blood pressure, relieves symptoms of discouragement, and more. But these are effects resulting from a transformed *heart*.

God is interested in our *hearts*. Are you giving grudgingly, only to "get"? Or are your gifts *overflowing* from a renewed spirit of delight and abundance?

*Lord, help me to give from a transformed heart, with the awareness that what I give, relationally and in every other way, will tend to be what I eventually receive.*

# WEEK 4
# Holy Hospitality

---

HOSPITALITY MEANS PRIMARILY THE CREATION OF FREE SPACE WHERE THE STRANGER CAN ENTER AND BECOME A FRIEND INSTEAD OF AN ENEMY. HOSPITALITY IS NOT TO CHANGE PEOPLE, BUT TO OFFER THEM SPACE WHERE CHANGE CAN TAKE PLACE.

– HENRI NOUWEN

---

# Open Eyes

**God saw all that he had made, and it was very good. Genesis 1:31a (NIV)**

Freddy dropped from my shoulders and hit the ground. My first precious grandson, who moments before had been happily riding on my back, was now on the ground crying. Instantly I imagined the worst. Could he have a concussion? Or something even more serious? As my son and daughter-in-law rushed him to the emergency room, I begged God for mercy, I cried, I shook. Although Freddy was later found to be fine, the shock of that moment took days to leave me. I tried to imagine life without this little child, and I just couldn't.

For weeks afterward, every time I held that little boy I was filled with inexpressible gratitude for his life, even more than I had felt before the accident. And something else happened to me: I became aware again of what someone has called "one of evil's most skilled secret agents: The agent of familiarity".

Our lives can become so *familiar* that we don't even realize we are surrounded by amazing gifts from God. Our own health, the beauty of trees and sunsets and stars, the friendship of loved ones, the way we are blessed to earn our daily bread, become almost invisible to us... until we're faced with the possible loss of something we were taking for granted.

Don't wait for the shock of a crisis. Today, think of blessings in your life (especially people) that you may not have noticed or thanked God for recently. Express your gratitude to God. And tell those people how much you love them.

Today's verse describes God seeing all that he had made, and observing that it is "very good." Can you be like God in this respect? Can you see, *really see*, all that God has made and see its goodness?

*Lord open my eyes to your blessings all around me! Help me not wait until a crisis to thank you for the wonderful gifts you have given me.*

# Who Is My Neighbor?

Part of hospitality to our neighbors means actually learning who our neighbors are!

In the space below, draw a simple diagram of your neighborhood, including the houses nearest yours. In squares representing each house, write the names of all your neighbors, including their children. Now write their occupations, and anything else of interest about them.

Most people are surprised to discover how little they know about their own neighbors. Make it your goal to fill in the blanks on your diagram, getting to know the people nearest you. And choose one or more neighbors to host at your house during this series! Simple hospitality, especially to people not exactly like you, is a path to so much healing and understanding.

# Refusing Riches

**"Then the master told his servant, 'Go out to the roads and country lanes and compel them to come in, so that my house will be full.'" Luke 14:23 (NIV) If you can, take time to read all of Luke 14:12-24**

In 2016, a highly regarded charity began an experimental program among the poorest of the poor in Kenya. Thousands of people were offered a basic income of one dollar a day. In Kenya's slums, this could literally change lives. They were free to use the money for anything they chose: Food, shelter, clothing, all in an effort to reduce poverty with less administrative overhead.

The experiment ran into unexpected trouble when many Kenyans... *refused the money*. In one region, 40% of the people offered this daily income refused it.

Investigations showed that people who refused the cash were skeptical. They found it "hard to believe that an organization would give roughly a year's salary in cash, unconditionally," the charity's director wrote in a letter to supporters. "As a result, many people created their own narratives to explain the cash, including rumors that the money is associated with cults or devil worship." He says the organization is considering cutting its losses and leaving that area in search of more welcoming regions.

Jesus told today's parable because something similar was happening to him: Many very religious people were declining to "come to the banquet" of grace he was offering, a relationship with God based on his grace, not on our scrupulous rule-keeping. Jesus explains, God is like a man who produces a beautiful, lavish banquet that is ready to enjoy – but none of his invited guests will come! So he sends out messengers and invites to his banquet anyone who is hungry—even the poorest of the poor.

There are two points of application for you and me: First, God extends his invitation to *everyone*. The banquet is free. But you and I have to choose to accept it.

Second: We are also the *messengers* that the rich man sends out! Each of us has a mission: To invite to the party anyone and everyone. Our mission is not to judge. Our mission is to invite.

Today, don't refuse any of the free gifts God is offering to you by his grace. And in your attitudes and actions and words, be like a messenger inviting people to a feast!

*Lord, help me see the free delights you are offering me today. May I not be too busy to notice, or too preoccupied to accept the invitation. And in all my interactions with others today, may my attitude be that of a messenger bearing invitations to a free banquet!*

# Hospitality to Strangers

**"When a foreigner resides among you in your land, do not mistreat them. The foreigner residing among you must be treated as your native-born. Love them as yourself, for you were foreigners in Egypt. I am the Lord your God." Leviticus 19:33-34 (NIV)**

In the Bible, offering hospitality, even to strangers, is actually a moral imperative. In today's passage, for example, the Israelites are told to love the "stranger" in their land as they love themselves. God later reminds them, "You are to love those who are foreigners, for you yourselves were foreigners in Egypt." (Deuteronomy 10:19)

In the Greek Scriptures, the word translated "hospitality" is a combination of the words *philos* meaning "brotherly love" and *xenos* meaning "stranger". It literally means "love strangers like family." The writer of Hebrews reminds us not to forget to "entertain strangers, for by so doing some people have entertained angels without knowing it." (Hebrews 13:2). The writer might be thinking of an episode in the book of Genesis, when Abraham offered hospitality to three strangers. It turned out he had entertained the Lord and two angels (Genesis 18:1-8)!

All these verses are meant to counteract the strong tendency to show hospitality only to our own tribe or family, or to those who might somehow benefit us. Jesus said, "When you give a banquet, invite the poor, the crippled, the lame, the blind, and you will be blessed. Although they cannot repay you, you will be repaid at the resurrection of the righteous." (Luke 14:13,14) Jesus is telling us to invite those on the outer margins of society to feast on both physical and spiritual food!

My friend and co-worker Valerie Webb has a great question every church should ask itself: "Are we a place that *gathers* people or a place that *sorts* people?" God is the only righteous judge. We can trust he will wisely sort the sheep from the goats one day. In the meantime, we invite everyone to gather in close and hear the Good News.

This is why outreaches like food banks ought to resonate deeply with Christians. Lavish generosity for the foreigner, the stranger, and the poor have been part of our DNA since the very beginning!

"Hospitality is making space for people that you don't have to make space for. In this, God is the inventor and lead actor. Creation was God making space for little creatures who were not necessary." — John Ortberg

*Lord, help me see how I can offer hospitality to those who are "strangers" to me. Help me to get over any timidity or hesitation and actually try it!*

# Reward for Hospitality

**"And if anyone gives even a cup of cold water to one of these little ones who is my disciple—truly I tell you, that person will not lose their reward." Matthew 10:42 (NIV)**

Some of my friends seem gifted with a talent for hospitality. Every meal they serve is an amazing feast, every conversation a delight, every room in their homes sparkles with creativity. On the other hand, there are those of us with great intentions to invite people over—then we think of what a mess the house is in, or we cringe to imagine serving guests the frozen skillet meals we cook for ourselves, or we suspect the conversation might stall or get awkward. Or we just get busy. So we put off hospitality endlessly.

God knows very well that we can get hesitant about showing hospitality. So Jesus ups the ante. He promises a *reward* for hospitality—even for something as basic as offering a cup of cold water! In Matthew 10, Jesus is teaching his disciples what to expect when they go out in his name. There will be rejection. But there will also be hospitality. And even the smallest act of kindness toward them will be noticed by God himself!

The wider application of the same principle is this: When you are considering showing hospitality, don't worry about preparing a Martha Stewart-worthy production. Just start simple. Can you offer a cup of water? Then invite someone over. And Jesus says, God will reward you!

You can schedule a meal or a cup of coffee (or water!) with someone today! Who will it be?

*Lord, help me be a host!*

# Practicing Hospitality

In the coming weeks invite (or join with one or two others to invite) someone to a meal meant to welcome and bless them. How you do that is up to you and creativity is encouraged, but the main thing is that you organize a moment in time for people to be shown love.

This might mean inviting someone in your neighborhood to a meal at your house. It might mean joining a group that feeds the poor or homeless. The aim of this project is to connect us more to the heart of our hospitable God.

I hope you will participate in the discussion on our Facebook page and share creative ideas... for example, inexpensive meals and recipes, or ways to start good conversations and break the ice!

# Hello Stranger

**Suppose a man comes into your meeting wearing a gold ring and fine clothes, and a poor man in filthy old clothes also comes in. If you show special attention to the man wearing fine clothes and say, "Here's a good seat for you," but say to the poor man, "You stand there" or "Sit on the floor by my feet," have you not discriminated among yourselves and become judges with evil thoughts? James 2:2-4 (NIV)**

Today at church I saw a visitor sitting in a pew at least 15 minutes before the service began (that's how I knew she must be a visitor! She was on time!). She was all alone. The clothes she wore, her hairstyle, and the color of her skin were typical of people from halfway around the world. I decided I would be intentional about making her feel very welcome, I even began to make my way toward her. But friends stopped to say hello. Staff members had questions. I got distracted. The worship music began. I realized I'd never made it to her, so I told myself I'd get over to say hello during the greeting time. But by the time I turned around later in the service, she was gone. And I never saw her again. Did she leave because she felt unwelcome and ignored? I may never know.

In today's verses, James is pointing out the tendency we all have of greeting only certain people in church, while walking right past others. His direct application has to do with showing favoritism to the rich. But favoritism can happen in any category: Favoritism for our friends, or for people we find amusing, or for anyone whose company we prefer to others. James says, "Not in church". When God's people gather, cast a hospitality net as wide as God's love.

Next time you see me in church, don't think me rude if I say, "Excuse me, I want to say hello to someone." I promise I won't think you're rude if you say that to me either! Let's all agree to make hospitality to the "stranger" our top priority!

*Heavenly Father, help me to make welcoming "strangers" a priority wherever I am, especially when the church gathers! Thank you for welcoming me into your presence!*

# The Neighbor Question

**For the entire law is fulfilled in keeping this one command: "Love your neighbor as yourself."**
**Galatians 5:14 (NIV)**

The dramatic tale of the Good Samaritan in Luke 10:30-37 is one of the most well-known of Jesus' parables. But its familiarity may give us the impression we know it better than we actually do. Here are some insights from research by Dr. John MacArthur. First, the context: Jesus is telling this story to a religious legalist who is trying to diminish the force of God's command to "love your neighbor" with a hairsplitting analysis of the word *neighbor*. "Wanting to justify himself, he asked Jesus, 'Who is my neighbor?'" (Luke 10:29).

In answer, Jesus tells a story that begins on the road "from Jerusalem to Jericho". I have traveled that road. Between those two cities, there's about a three-thousand-foot drop over 17 miles, and in places the roadside hangs over precipitous cliffs hundreds of feet high. The road is lined with caves and boulders. It's a perfect path for bandits.

In Jesus' story, a Jewish man traveling alone on this road is jumped by thieves and not only robbed but stripped, severely beaten, and left for dead. Then: hope! Jesus says, "A priest came down that road." But the priest "passed by on the other side." Then a Levite comes by (Levites were considered the most "religious" tribe of Israel and often held prestigious jobs in the temple). But as soon as he sees the man lying there, he also crosses over to the other side.

Then along comes a Samaritan. In Jesus' time there was deep racial and religious hostility between Jews and Samaritans. But this Samaritan sees a Jewish man, his blood enemy, on the road dying. And he has compassion. He bandages his wounds and brings him to an inn. He leaves two denarii for the innkeeper to pay for the man's recovery (that was enough for two months of room and board!). He had never met the man. He does not investigate before he helps. He does not subject him to cross-examination. In other words, he never stops to ask the question, "Am I this man's neighbor?" He just helps.

At the end of the story Jesus turns the religious leader's question back at him: "So, which of these three do you think was a neighbor to the man who was attacked by the thieves?" Notice how Jesus flips the question: It's no longer *"Who is my neighbor?"* but *"To whom will I be a neighbor?"*

This parable is more than a mandate for humanitarianism. I hope you are motivated that way, but there's a deeper lesson here: The way the Good Samaritan showed care for the traveler is the way God loves you! It's when we realize that, spiritually, we've all been in the position of the dying man— and were rescued by the grace of God—that we are then well-motivated to be a loving neighbor to those around us!

*God, help me see all those I meet as my neighbor. Help me to be truly "neighborly" to all.*

# WEEK 5

# My Source of Security

---

STARE AT JESUS LONG ENOUGH
AND YOU WILL BECOME A GIVER.
GIVE LONG ENOUGH AND YOU WILL
BECOME LIKE CHRIST.
- RANDY ALCORN

---

# Jesus is the Source

**For you know the grace of our Lord Jesus Christ, that though he was rich, yet for your sake he became poor, so that you by his poverty might become rich. 2 Corinthians 8:9 (ESV)**

The anonymous author of *Overflow: A Life Refreshed by Generosity* writes, "Jesus is THE generosity story that trumps all generosity stories. He is our model and motivator of whole-life generosity. If we have a generosity story to tell, it's because of his story. Our story revolves around his story. Our stories only faintly point to his greater story."

Generosity with Jesus at the center is a cycle: The more we realize how gracious God has been to us through Christ, the more we are motivated to be generous to others. The more generous we are, the more like Christ we become. The more like Christ we become, the more generous we want to be!

The *Overflow* author suggests a mental exercise: Imagine generosity like a majestic fountain where an unlimited supply of water flows up from the source (Jesus), through the fountain (you), overflowing the basin into other people's lives. As they are refreshed, they give gratitude to God, and as they live in greater awareness of God's grace, they become generous themselves. And as you see how they are refreshed, you are blessed yourself and even more motivated to be generous!

People sometimes think of generosity as the act of giving something away––a net loss. But biblical generosity is a way of thinking and of being that results in joy and blessing. A life of generosity with Jesus at the center is not draining. It's refreshing and replenishing. That is God's promise!

*Lord, help me see myself as a fountain supplied endlessly by you, the source!*

TLC

## TUESDAY
# The Color of Money

**"What does it profit a man to gain the whole world, but lose his own soul?" Mark 8:36**

There's a topic Jesus talked about more than heaven, more than prayer, more than faith, more than sin...the topic of money. Sixteen out of 38 parables he told were about money and possessions. In the entire New Testament there are some 500 verses on prayer, but over 2,000 about money. Why? God knows it can be a blessing or a curse. To be more precise, *the way money is used* can be a curse or a blessing. Both to you and to others.

I think of it this way: U.S. paper money is green, the color of growth and new life. And money *will* make things grow; *what* it grows depends on where you direct it.

Imagine all your resources as a source of energy that you direct to whatever you want to flourish. As pastor Sherman Smith puts it, if you take your money or time or talents and share them with, say, a person in need or a school or a church, you are pouring energy into those things and saying, "grow and flourish." If you take your resources and direct them toward unholy things—vices in your life, for example, or imagined fears, or time spent with media that makes you angry—you are in essence giving energy there and saying, "grow and flourish."

What is it that you would like to grow? people

*Heavenly Father, help me use all my resources—my words, my time, my talents, my money—to help good things grow.*

# Secure Deposits

**"Do not store up for yourselves treasures on earth, where moth and rust destroy and where thieves break in and steal. But store up for yourselves treasures in heaven, where moth and rust do not destroy, and thieves do not break in and steal." Matthew 6:19-20 (NIV)**

If you're not careful, it's easy to misread what Jesus is saying here. Why does Jesus tell his followers not to "store up treasures on earth"? Because treasures are bad? *No! Because they won't last—if stored that way.* Jesus is not even saying "do not store up treasures." In fact he *wants* us to store up treasure. He's just telling us to stop storing our wealth in places that ultimately are an insecure investment.

Randy Alcorn gives this illustration: Imagine you're alive at the end of the Civil War. You're a Northern secret agent in the South and have lots of Confederate money. Suppose you know the North will soon win. What will you do with all your Confederate dollars? If you're smart, you'll exchange it all ASAP for United States currency. Because when the war ends, all your Confederate money will be worthless.

In the same way, you and I only have a limited time on earth. US dollars (or Swiss francs or Euro dollars or any other currency) are no good in the afterlife. You can't take it with you. So, Jesus says, exchange your currency into something that has value where you're headed. By using our resources for God's work, Jesus says we're in effect trading the unstable money of this world for the eternal treasure of heaven.

Think of life this way, as a dot with a line following it that goes on forever:

The dot represents our lives here on earth; the line, our lives with God forever after we die. Most people live life for the dot. *Live for the line.*

As Oswald Smith said, "You can't take it with you—but you can send it on ahead."

*Lord, help me always consider how to best invest for eternity! Show me an opportunity to be generous today. I am watching and listening for it.*

# Where is My Hope?

**Command those who are rich in this present world not to be arrogant nor to put their hope in wealth, which is so uncertain, but to put their hope in God, who richly provides us with everything for our enjoyment. Command them to do good, to be rich in good deeds, and to be generous and willing to share. In this way they will lay up treasure for themselves as a firm foundation for the coming age, so that they may take hold of the life that is truly life. 1 Timothy 6:17-19 (NIV)**

One of the more controversial statements of Jesus in our culture (and in his) is in Luke 18:24-25: "It is easier for a camel to go through the eye of a needle than for someone who is rich to enter the kingdom of God."

So what's his point? Jesus is not saying wealth is not a blessing. He's saying it's so easy for us to move from seeing wealth as God's blessing to seeing wealth *as a god*. That happens subtly. All the things God wants me to trust him for—peace, security, fulfillment, provision, self-esteem, hope—I begin to trust money to provide.

Maybe you're thinking, "Well, I'm not rich, so this verse doesn't apply to me. Dodged a bullet!" Check this out: Just before I wrote today's devotional I went to a web site, GlobalRichList. com. It collects no personal identifying information. You just plug in your approximate annual income and it calculates your rank in the list of the world's wealthiest people. I entered my income and was stunned at the result. Try it! Are you surprised?

After you've discovered where you rank on the global rich list, try this exercise suggested in the book *Overflow: A Life Refreshed by Generosity*. Look at the verse at the top of the page and plug in your name:

" _____Fran_____, do not put your hope in wealth, which is so uncertain, but put your hope in God, who richly provides you with everything for your enjoyment. _____Fran_____, do good, be rich in good deeds, be generous and willing to share. In this way, _____money_____, you will lay up treasure in heaven!"

Of all the phrases in that verse, which one challenges you the most personally?

Here are some fun ways to live out that verse: I heard someone talk about developing "generosity radar". That means their eyes are open to the multiple ways they can show generosity every day—even with just a smile or friendly wave.

Another couple I know sets aside a small amount from every paycheck as "random giving money"—if they see a need, they can have fun filling it for other people! They have paid for people's meals, given car wash coupons, provided oil changes, bought clothes for others—all because they enjoy it, and have set aside some cash for this little hobby of theirs. And they are not rich people! They're just generous people.

I love the way Eugene Cho summarizes a principle in this verse: *"Generosity is what keeps the things we own from owning us."*

*God, help me follow this verse, developing "generosity radar" for others!*

# Hoard it or Share it

**"A certain rich man thought to himself, 'What shall I do? I have no place to store my crops.' Then he said, 'This is what I'll do. I will tear down my barns and build bigger ones, and there I will store my surplus grain. And I'll say to myself, "You have plenty of grain laid up for many years. Take life easy; eat, drink and be merry."' But God said to him, 'You fool! This very night your life will be demanded from you. Then who will get what you have prepared for yourself?'" Luke 12:17-20 (NIV)**

"Oseola McCarty spent a lifetime making other people look nice." So begins the *New York Times* article about this remarkable woman. Day after day, for most of her 87 years, Oseola took in bundles of dirty clothes and laundered them. The *Times* article goes on: "She spent almost nothing, living in her old family home, cutting the toes out of shoes if they did not fit right and binding her ragged Bible with Scotch tape to keep Corinthians from falling out."

So it surprised everyone when in 1995, five years before her death, Oseola fully funded a perpetual scholarship for black women like herself at the University of Southern Mississippi. People at the school call her donation The Gift. She made the $150,000 donation (worth a quarter million today) in anticipation of her death. In an interview with the *Times*, she said, "I know it won't be too many years before I pass on, and I just figured the money would do them a lot more good than it would me." She insisted that her life was not hard: "I live where I want to live, and I live the way I want to live," she said. "I just wanted to do this. I planned to do this."

People who have learned to live with whole-life generosity look at the world in full awareness that they will not live forever. They ask, "How can I find effective ways to make my wealth live on by giving some of it away?" Others look at the world without considering the brevity of life and ask, "How can I preserve my wealth for myself?" That's what the rich man in this parable did. Jesus points out the obvious: When we're gone, what we have stored for ourselves will belong to others anyway. So direct it intentionally now, before you go.

Ask yourself: How am I spreading my resources so that I will leave a legacy for others when I am gone?

*Lord, I want to leave a legacy. I want to leave behind me a wake of goodness that impacts lives for generations, in ways I may never have imagined in this life. Help me to do so!*

## SATURDAY
# The Link Between Risk and Generosity

**(Jesus said) "The children of this world are more shrewd in dealing with the world around them than are the children of the light." Luke 16:8B (NLT)**

Psychologist Richard Wiseman has done fascinating work on *luck*. Is it true that some people are just lucky, while others are unlucky? Over the course of 10 years, Wiseman followed the lives of 400 subjects of all ages and professions (he found them after he placed ads in newspapers asking for people who thought of themselves as very lucky or very unlucky). He had them keep diaries and perform tests.

He discovered that the "lucky" tended to risk more, putting themselves more often in situations where anything could happen. The "lucky" try more things, and fail more often, but when they fail they shrug it off and try something else. Because they try more stuff, it's more probable that exciting things will happen to them.

"Unlucky" people tend to crave security and to be more anxious, so instead of wading into the sea of random chance, they remain fixated on controlling the situation. As a result, they miss out on the thousands of opportunities that float by.

His research reminds me of the most surprising parables Jesus told; about shrewd money managers who take risks, invest their masters' cash (sometimes in shady deals), and get personal rewards. And Jesus commends them! What's he getting at? I think he was pointing out how people of the "world" are often willing to be aggressive and take chances with their investments because they hope for a payoff, while people of faith often prize conservative, low-risk behavior. But Jesus is critical of those who never take risks. If we're afraid to risk anything, very little good will be accomplished.

Jesus told a parable specifically about these two kinds of

people: The parable of the talents. The ending haunts me. After two servants take risks with their master's resources and report a profit on their investments, "the last servant said, 'Master, I know you have high standards…I was afraid I might disappoint you, so I found a good hiding place and secured your money. Here it is, safe and sound down to the last cent.' The master was furious. 'That's a terrible way to live! It's criminal to live cautiously like that!'" (Matthew 25:24-27 TM)

Do you tend to demonstrate "adventurous generosity," or do you tend to stay conservative with your giving, perhaps because you frame your life experience with a sense of scarcity? True confession: That latter category is the one I naturally fall into. But I have discovered that generosity—for the kingdom of God—is rewarding! That's something I have grown into, not something I was born with.

*Lord, help me remember that failure is not the greatest risk. The greatest risk is never trying.*

# WEEK 6

# My Resources and God's Power

---

GIVE WHAT YOU CAN.

TO SOMEONE, IT MAY BE BETTER

THAN YOU DARE TO THINK.

– HENRY WADSWORTH LONGFELLOW

---

# Live in Richness

**Now all praise to God for his wonderful kindness to us and his favor that he has poured out upon us because we belong to his dearly loved Son. So overflowing is his kindness toward us that he took away all our sins through the blood of his Son, by whom we are saved; and he has showered down upon us the richness of his grace... Ephesians 1:6-8a (TLB)**

Homer and Langley Collyer were wealthy. They lived in a mansion on Fifth Avenue in New York City. Yet inside their house, the reclusive brothers lived as paupers. They ate only oranges. They never cleaned. When they died in 1947, it took authorities weeks to find their bodies, so filled with trash was their multi-million dollar property.

Sometimes we believers are like the Collyers. Spiritually wealthy. Privileged. Resourced. Yet we live in the collected garbage of our past, not really enjoying the blessings that surround us—or even aware of them. How conscious are you daily of the blessings that are yours? In the busyness of modern life, do you subsist on a paltry spiritual diet when rich food is yours for the taking?

Slow down. Look again at today's verses. Note the words Paul uses to describe God's blessings: "kindness...favor...richness... grace..." Now look at the words he uses to describe the way God gives us these blessings: "poured out...overflowing... showered down upon us..." God is not a stingy gift-giver. He is lavish, generous, prodigal in the way he treats you and me.

God lavished his riches on you before you were even born. And his gift-giving did not stop there. I guarantee that even today he will give you a beautiful gift: The gift of someone's love, an unexpected kindness, a word of encouragement, a beautiful vista, a reminder of his grace given in Christ. Keep your eyes open today—and enjoy the gifts he gives to you!

*God, I don't want to live like a spiritual miser. Help me enjoy the lavish spiritual blessings you have given that surround me every day!*

# Little into Much

**Jesus took the five loaves and two fish, looked up toward heaven, and blessed them. Then, breaking the loaves into pieces, he kept giving the bread and fish to the disciples so they could distribute it to the people. They all ate as much as they wanted, and afterward, the disciples picked up twelve baskets of leftovers! Luke 9:16-17 (NLT)**

The "Feeding of the Five Thousand" is one of the few miracles recorded in all four gospels, so it obviously made quite an impression. Jesus took five bread buns and two sardines from a child's lunch and turned them into a feast.

Have you learned that God can take the little we give and turn it into much? The church I serve, Twin Lakes Church, is a great example. TLC was started back in 1890, but completely closed for over eight years from 1922 to 1930. It was a leaky shell of a building. Shuttered. Dead.

Then on March 30, 1930– and we still have the handwritten minutes of this amazing meeting— seven women and five men met to restart the church. Shortly afterward, when these eleven people had paid all the outstanding bills, they recorded the grand total left in the church bank account that day: 19 cents.

For a while I kept a dime, a nickel, and four pennies in my pocket to remind myself of this modern loaves-and-fishes example. *Eleven people. 19 cents*. That's all they had. But they gave it. And God did something amazing.

It staggers my mind when I think of all that sprang from that seed. Tens of thousands of people have attended TLC since March 30, 1930. Hundreds who found faith there have gone on to lead other churches and missions and schools and clinics and non-profits as pastors or lay leaders. Out of Twin Lakes has grown a successful camp, preschool, grade school, junior high school, after-school day care, food pantry, internet ministry, new churches, and countless thousands of hours given to local and foreign ministries and agencies. Every building on our property has a sister building in the developing world, representing churches and orphanages and clinics and schools all over the planet.

*But without the willingness of those 11 people and their 19 cents, none of that would have happened.* They planted a tiny seed. People who followed them watered. And God made it all grow.

World changers put their little bit into play and then wait to see what happens. What do you have, what can you give? Encouragement? Volunteering? Prayer?

Impact. It's not about what you have. It's about what you do with what you have. Or more precisely, what God does with what you are willing to give. *Stop doubting your ability to contribute. Stop doubting your opportunity to make a difference.* Give the Lord your lunch. And watch as he produces a never-ending banquet of grace.

*God, I confess there are times I feel I don't have much to give. Help me remember ways you've turned little into much in my life already. Help me give what I can and trust you for the rest.*

# The Source of It All

**You may say to yourself, "My power and the strength of my hands have produced this wealth for me." But remember the Lord your God, for it is he who gives you the ability to produce wealth, and so confirms his covenant, which he swore to your ancestors, as it is today. Deuteronomy 8:17-18 (NIV)**

God is the creator of everything. So whenever we use the resources of this world, we are using resources God made in the first place.

How can living each day in the awareness that God owns everything change the way you experience life? How can it change your perspective, the way you shop, the way you look at your job, the way you look at your family, the way you give?

Today as you drive your car or enjoy a meal or relax in your home, thank God for the use of all these things that he ultimately owns!

"God doesn't really need our money, as if he needed an income. Instead, we need him every moment to sustain us." –Andrew Field

*Thank you, God. You are ultimately the source of all I see that is good: My resources, my home and family, the sunshine, the greenery, the beloved friends, the poor wanderers who need food and shelter. Help me care for it all as your steward.*

# Where Your Treasure is...

**For where your treasure is, there your heart will be also.**
**Matthew 6:21 (NIV)**

When my wife and I were considering buying Apple stock, we instantly developed a fascination for that company: We checked the Wall Street Journal for articles, we studied magazine pieces about Apple, we evangelized friends with demonstrations of how awesome our iPhones and iPads were. And the same thing has happened since we began investing our time and resources into a children's home in India. Every article about India now catches our attention. Every person we meet from India fascinates us. Anyone with a connection to orphanages in the developing world is an instant friend and source of knowledge.

Here's the principle: Investment leads; the heart follows. As Jesus said, "For where your treasure is, there your heart will be also."

Do you wish you cared more about eternal things? Do you wish you prayed more often for the spiritual growth of the next generation instead of just complaining about where the world is headed? Do you wish your heart was more tender toward the poor or the homeless? Jesus tells you exactly what to do: Put your resources in ministries that serve those areas and your heart will follow. Your prayer life will change. Your thought life will change.

And by the way, that's what God wants, more than your money: Your heart. As one writer puts it, "He isn't looking for 'donors'. He's looking for disciples."

This helps explain Jesus' sometimes confusing stance toward the wealthy. He tells the rich young ruler in Luke 18:22, "Sell all you have and give the money to the poor." The young man walks away sadly. Just a few verses later, the wealthy Zaccheus proclaims he'll give half his belongings to the poor. And Jesus is delighted! So why does Jesus ask for 100% from one guy and just 50% from the next? Because he isn't giving us a one-size-fits-all set of rules to memorize. He is trying to do something *inside* of us. He wants us to *internalize* and *personalize* this issue.

And he knows this is the best path to a richer life. Harvard Business School professor Michael Norton and University of British Columbia psychology professor Elizabeth Dunn decided to scientifically study the question, *Can money buy happiness?* They found that it can... *as long as we spend it on others*. The book *Love Let Go* summarizes their research: People were happier when they gave money away. They found these conclusions to hold true all over the world, in country after country.

So when Jesus tells us to store up treasures in heaven by giving them away, he's not commanding some kind of buzzkill penance. He's actually saying, believe me, this is the best value you can get for your money.

God is looking for people whose imaginations have been captured by what moves his heart. Because those are people through whom God changes the world.

*Lord, help me see where my heart really is right now... and thereby see where my treasure truly lies. Help me invest my treasure where I would like to grow my heart!*

# FRIDAY
# Not Mine

**The earth is the Lord's, and everything in it. Psalm 24:1 (NIV)**

**Remember the LORD your God, for it is he who gives you the ability to produce wealth. Deuteronomy 8:18a (NIV)**

When writing today's meditation, I was surprised to see best-selling author Randy Alcorn (whom I've quoted several times in this devotional) enjoying ice cream with his grandson in a local café! I told him about this book and he grew very excited, because generosity is his passion.

Randy is an exceptional person. He now gives away nearly everything he makes, including book royalties, and lives on a very limited income. He wrote what I think is the best short book on generosity, *The Treasure Principle*, based on his experiences. Here's the main idea from which all his actions flow: *"God owns everything. I'm his money manager."*

The biblical word for a money manager was *steward*. In the ancient world it was common for stewards to invest their master's money and take care of their property. Stewards had total autonomy to make decisions on behalf of the master, but were expected to show a profit when their master returned, sometimes after years away. Jesus often told parables about how *we* are stewards of God's resources.

In his book, Alcorn tells the story of his friend Jerry Caven. He owned a successful restaurant chain, two banks, lots of commercial real estate, a large ranch, and a farm. He had never given more than token amounts to charity. When Jerry approached retirement, he sought a nice lakeside retirement home. But God unexpectedly nudged his heart in another direction. Jerry now spends a lot of time in India with ministries he generously helps there. He says the concept that activated his generosity was *stewardship*: "Once my wife and I understood that we were giving away *God's* money to do God's work, we discovered a peace and joy we never had back when we thought of it as *our* money!"

I agree with Randy: Whenever I start thinking like an *owner*, it's a red flag to me. I am a *steward* of everything in my life: The bank account with my name on it, the house I live in, even the people in my family and the church I serve—none of them are mine to keep forever. I am stewarding those precious resources for Someone Else. Interestingly, I find that when I think of myself as a *steward* of my resources, I end up managing them in ways much more beneficial to me than when I think of myself as an *owner*!

*Father, help me always to think of myself as your steward, your resource manager. Help me to manage your stuff wisely!*

# The Law of the Harvest

**Whoever sows sparingly will also reap sparingly, and whoever sows generously will also reap generously. 2 Corinthians 9:6 (NIV)**

I was traveling through the second poorest nation in the Western hemisphere, Nicaragua, with my friend Rigo. He'd been an executive at Dole Foods before becoming a full-time supervisor of pastors in the country. He was taking me to a rural village, one of the poorest he had ever seen. It's not on any map. He had only stumbled into it when he got lost the year before.

The villagers there were starving when he found them. Their one crop, corn, was growing horribly stunted and shriveled. They couldn't sell it at market, so they had no money for anything—their cows and chickens were all starving. When Rigo asked if they were interested in starting a church there, the villagers told him, "Why? Even God has abandoned us."

So Rigo decided to call in some favors from his old contacts at Dole. He got the very best commercial corn seed and taught the villagers how to grow it. When I visited the village with him one year later, it was quite literally overflowing with the harvest: Their makeshift silos were all full, so they were storing corn in their own homes. I saw ears of corn pouring out of doors and windows, piles and piles of them. I heard chickens clucking happily in their modern, clean, humane coops (also procured by Rigo). The villagers told me, "Rigo thinks he got lost that day, but the truth is, God heard our cry and sent him to us!" They started a church, their very first. On the Sunday I visited, it was filled with praises. They told me, "We are now rich! We want to give so that other villages can be rich too."

Their experience echoes one of the deepest Bible passages on generosity: "Whoever sows sparingly will also reap sparingly, and whoever sows generously will also reap generously... Now he who supplies seed to the sower and bread for food will also supply and increase your store of seed and will enlarge the harvest of your righteousness. You will be enriched in every way so that you can be generous on every occasion, and through us your generosity will result in thanksgiving to God." (2 Cor. 9:6,10-11)

Paul is restating the "Law of the Harvest": Generally speaking, what you get out of life is related to what you give away. This is not some holy get-rich-quick scheme. We don't give *in order* to get rich. But the general principle is true: If we sow (that's another word for planting seeds), we will reap (another word for harvesting crops). And the more we sow, the more we will reap. Then we can keep giving from our harvest. And the cycle continues!

The corollaries are also true:  **You reap *what* you sow.** If you plant corn seeds, you don't expect to reap cucumbers. If you want to harvest great ministry in your local church, or great relationships in your family, you need to invest in it.

**You reap *later* than you sow.** Don't give up if the harvest doesn't come in one day.

**You reap *more than* you sow.**  No farmer would plant corn seed if he thought he would get one corn seed back. When you give your time or resources, don't think of it as a *loss*. Think of it as *seed sown*. There will be a harvest.

*Lord, help me to see myself as a sower. Help me see that I am planting seeds for the future in every conversation and in every contribution!*

# WEEK 7
# Inside-Out Generosity

WHEN WE GIVE CHEERFULLY

AND ACCEPT GRATEFULLY,

EVERYONE IS BLESSED.

- MAYA ANGELOU

# Generosity Models

**All the believers were one in heart and mind. No one claimed that any of their possessions was their own, but they shared everything they had. With great power the apostles continued to testify to the resurrection of the Lord Jesus. And God's grace was so powerfully at work in them all that there were no needy persons among them. Acts 4:32-34a (NIV)**

Joyful generosity is always better caught than taught. So think of the most generous people you have known. What were they like?

I think of my own Mom. From the time my father died when I was nearly four years old and my sister was just one-and-a-half, to the time I was in junior high, Mom raised us as a single woman. Our income put us below the national poverty line. Yet she was one of the most giving people I have ever known. She was generous with her time, her love, her service to others, and our money (when she was giving to others. Within our own household, thriftiness was a high value! I used to think Mom was just cheap until it dawned on me that she pinched pennies in order to give them away).

Although we often ate food distributed by the local rescue mission and wore clothes bought at thrift stores, she found ways to be generous with our very limited resources. She taught my sister and me that generosity really is a mindset that is completely independent of wealth. She modeled how to live very frugally and yet to make doing God's work a top priority. I was surprised to learn when she passed away that she had been on the donor rolls of many well-known charities and ministries. Generosity was in her DNA.

It reminds me of what Paul said about the Macedonian Christians. Three things contributed to making them generous: Their severe trial, their extreme poverty, and their overflowing joy (2 Cor. 8:1,2). They gave because they themselves knew what a blessing such gifts could be!

The early Christians in Acts 4 are another great model for us to follow in their generosity, because it flowed naturally and joyfully out of a sense of gratitude toward God. No one forced them to give. Yet they created an atmosphere where generosity was the air they breathed.

Who are your generosity models? What inspiration do you get from their lives?

*Father, thank you for these generosity models in my life:*

*May I be more like them, and become a generosity model to others!*

# Generosity is Contagious

**(Jesus said) "Let your light shine before others, so that they may see your good works and give glory to your Father who is in heaven." Matthew 5:16 (ESV)**

The catalyst was a kindergartner.

Five-year old Travis Beuse was sick one Sunday and sat with his mom and the other grown-ups in "big church" instead of his usual class. That meant he heard my description of our local food bank—and it captured his imagination as it had captured mine.

I told the congregation how Second Harvest Food Bank literally *banks* food—fresh produce and more—in their huge warehouse, and then distributes it to dozens of local agencies, mostly churches and faith-based soup kitchens, to give to the needy.

Later that day Travis told his mother Katrina he had made several paper kites to sell door-to-door in his neighborhood to raise money for the hungry. His mom felt extremely awkward, especially since she herself was a single mom without much to give. But Travis insisted, so door to door they went, for about an hour. Katrina thought, "Well, at least that's over," but, bolstered by his success, Travis made more kites each day, and dragged Mom to more neighborhoods. At one home she took a picture of him selling his kites and emailed it to me. And I showed it the next week in church.

The rest is history. Inspired by Travis, the congregation gave joyfully and spontaneously and within three weeks had contributed over a *quarter million dollars* for the food bank, enough to provide over *one million meals*, apparently the largest donation any church had made to a food bank in America to that point. To put this in perspective, in 2016 the largest fast-food chain on the planet, Subway, generously gave a total of one million meals to Feeding America, a network of food banks.

But the story here is not that one local church out-gave a multinational corporation. The story is that it was all inspired by a *kindergartner*.

This is what happens when you give: It's inspiring. Your light shines and others are inspired—not only to give, but to give glory to God. You and I have no idea what avalanche of generosity our small snowflake may be tipping into motion. I've since had several new attenders to our church tell me they first heard of our congregation through a news story about that food bank donation.

Some may object, "But didn't Jesus tell us to give in secret?" He told us not to give *in order to be seen* (Matthew 6:1). In other words, if your giving is a way for you to boost your personal ego or status, there's something amiss. This frees us from any external pressure to give.

But Jesus also said, "Let your light shine before others, that they may see your good deeds and praise your Father in heaven." (Matthew 5:16).

Think about it. How will a new Christian or a young person learn about the joy and the blessing of giving? In a tactful way, when appropriate, role models of generosity are so important. Contagious, joyful, child-like generosity creates a domino effect that changes the world!

*Lord, help me to give in a way that is joyful and contagious!*

# I Would Take More Risks

**"The man who had received five bags of gold went at once and put his money to work and gained five bags more. So also, the one with two bags of gold gained two more. Then the man who had received one bag of gold ...said, 'I was afraid and went out and hid your gold in the ground.'"**
**Matthew 25:16,17,25 (NIV)**

Psychologist Richard Leider spent decades interviewing senior citizens. He asked just one question: "If you had to live your life over again, what would you do differently?" Their advice consistently boiled down to three things:

1. *They would be more reflective.*

2. *They would take more risks.*

3. *They would try to understand what really gave them fulfillment.* Not what gave them a momentary buzz or what made them feel pleasure but what made them truly fulfilled, on the soul level. And then they would do those things more.

In the parable of the talents, Jesus is urging his disciples to do exactly those three things. The wise servants are commended for taking more risks and investing in what truly brings fulfillment: pleasing God. Jesus is saying, risk-taking for God will always be rewarded; if not on earth, then certainly in heaven! He has given you resources. Leverage them for his work.

*Father, help me to be more reflective about the big picture of my life and its purpose. Help me to take more risks for you. Help me to spend my time on what really brings soul-deep fulfillment, not just momentary pleasure or distraction. Thank you!*

# The Benefits of Giving

**The Lord Jesus himself said: "It is more blessed to give than to receive." Acts 20:35b**

Jesus said something about generosity that may surprise you: It's in your own best interest!

Scientists studying the effects of altruism agree. Rachel Swalin, writing for Health.com, summarizes several academic studies:

- A 2006 study in the *International Journal of Psychophysiology* found generosity lowers blood pressure.
- A study in the *Journal of Health Psychology* concluded generosity reduces stress.
- A 2013 study of 846 people published in *American Journal of Public Health* found that very generous people live, in general, substantially longer than average.

Generosity has also been shown to boost your mood, promote social connections, and improve the quality of your marriage.

The University of Notre Dame has an entire academic center on the science of generosity. Two of their researchers, Christian Smith and Hilary Davidson, report in their book *The Paradox of Generosity* that Americans who donate more than 10 percent of their incomes have lower depression rates. Those who are relationally generous (forgiving, empathetic, hospitable) are far more likely to be in "excellent health" than those who are not. Americans who volunteer an average of 5.8 hours a week describe themselves as "very happy", while those who only volunteer 0.6 hours per week label themselves "unhappy".

As Laura Sumner Truax and Amalya Campbell put it in their excellent book *Love Let Go: Radical Generosity for the Real World*, "All of us have a super-power capable of improving almost every aspect of our lives. We flourish when we use this power. And those around us flourish as well. When we this power. And those around us flourish as well. When we use this power, studies show, we have increased energy and happiness. These results are as conclusive as the link between exercise and health. Equally amazing is that most of us simply don't believe it. What is this super-power? *Generosity.*"

Paul says of the Corinthians' generous gifts to the poor, "This benefits you... you will be enriched in every way to be further generous in every way, which will result in even more thanksgiving to God." (2 Corinthians 9:11)

John Ortberg observes, "When you give, it sets a divine, supernatural process in motion that enriches not only the people that receive what you give, it enriches you. When people's hearts become captivated by the desire to give, God enables them to give in ways they could not have anticipated, their lives become adventures in giving, and they overflow with joy."

Remember the promise: "God loves the cheerful giver. And God will generously provide all you need." (2 Cor. 9:7-8) It truly is more blessed to give than to receive!

"We should see giving like a roller coaster ride: it feels adventurous and risky, but it's really safe. And anything that fun becomes contagious!" –Andrew Field

*Father, help me see giving as a thrill ride that is fun and actually good for me!*

# It Can Happen Again

**"Live such good lives among the pagans that, though they accuse you of doing wrong, they may see your good deeds and glorify God..." 1 Peter 2:12 (NIV)**

Author and pastor Andy Stanley points out that one of the most compelling arguments for the Christian faith is the simple fact that it *survived*. The odds against it were incredible. "For nearly three centuries," he writes, "Christians remained utterly powerless--ostracized socially, persecuted politically, and tortured physically. Yet somehow their movement continued to grow. How?"

University of Washington sociologist Rodney Stark examined the perplexing growth of early Christianity from a historical perspective in his seminal book *The Rise of Christianity*. He reached a fascinating conclusion. He believed its appeal can be traced to a simple characteristic: Generosity.

Stark describes how several plagues ripped through the cities of the ancient Roman Empire, and each time the people would flee to the countryside to escape disease, leaving the sick with no one to care for them. Except Christians.

Some of those Romans even wrote about their experiences with early Christians. One of the surviving accounts is by a man named Pachomius. When the Roman army conquered his city and conscripted him as a soldier, he was thrown into prison along with other young draftees so they couldn't run away before training camp. Then a sudden epidemic raced through the region and the jailers fled, leaving the prisoners to starve.

But Pachomius writes that strangers began showing up at night, slipping food through prison bars. Night after night these mysterious benefactors returned. Pachomius and all his friends survived. Questions burned in his mind for years: *Who were those people? Why did they help us?*

When he got out of the army, he decided to investigate. People in town told him those midnight visitors had been part of a group known variously as Galileans, Followers of The

When he got out of the army, he decided to investigate. People in town told him those midnight visitors had been part of a group known variously as Galileans, Followers of The Way... or *Christians*. Pachomius discovered where they met, soon became a Christian himself, and eventually matured into a great leader in the Jesus movement. His experience is just one of thousands of similar stories. People were drawn to the Christians because of their *generosity*.

Generosity still captures the imaginations of people today.

*New York Times* writer Nicholas Kristof, an atheist and frequent critic of religious excess, has written several columns describing what he admires about Christians: Their generosity. In a March 29, 2015 column, Kristof writes, "I have little in common, politically or theologically, with evangelicals... but I've been truly awed by those I've seen in so many remote places, combating illiteracy and warlords, famine and disease, humbly struggling to do the Lord's work as they see it..."

Kristof then shares the story of Dr. Stephen Foster, a Christian missionary who has given his life to care for the poor and sick in Angola. So sincere and selfless is the work of Dr. Foster and his colleagues that it has redefined Kristof's idea of Christianity: "I must say that a disproportionate share of the aid workers I've met in the wildest places over the years, long after anyone sensible had evacuated, have been evangelicals, nuns or priests. In the U.S., the safety net of soup kitchens, food pantries and women's shelters depends heavily on religious donations and volunteers." And remember, he says this as an atheist.

What if the church worldwide became known once again for inexplicable, daring, sacrificial generosity?

"Our generosity sends a message about the God we believe in, a God who loved so much he *gave*—no strings attached. He didn't take. He gave. That's grace. And the best object lesson of that *theology* is our *generosity*." –Andy Stanley

*God, thank you for extending your generosity to me. Thank you for the inspiring example of the first Christ-followers. Help me to be a part of it happening again!*

# The Joy of Giving

**But Zacchaeus stood up and said to the Lord, "Look, Lord! Here and now I give half of my possessions to the poor, and if I have cheated anybody out of anything, I will pay back four times the amount." Jesus said to him, "Today salvation has come to this house, because this man, too, is a son of Abraham." Luke 19:8,9**

I love Charles Dickens' classic tale *A Christmas Carol*. When the story starts, Ebenezer Scrooge is stingy, greedy, selfish, fearful, and miserable. But after three ghosts show him the effects both of generosity and of stinginess, he's a changed man. He wakes up with joy on Christmas morning, and here's how Dickens describes the new wonder he finds in the world around him:

> He went to church, and walked about the streets, and watched the people hurrying to and fro, and patted children on the head, and questioned beggars, and looked down into the kitchens of houses, and up to the windows, and found that everything could yield him pleasure. He had never dreamed that any walk—that anything—could give him so much happiness.

He buys the Cratchit family a turkey and brings children toys and donates to a collection for the poor. And on the story's final page, Dickens writes of Scrooge:

> Some people laughed to see the alteration in him, but he let them laugh, and little heeded them... His own heart laughed, and that was quite enough for him. And it was always said of him, that he knew how to keep Christmas well, if any man alive possessed the knowledge.

Randy Alcorn points out that Scrooge was giddy with delight on those London streets because he found the antidote to fear and materialistic anxieties: Joyful giving. His joy echoes the pleasure Zacchaeus finds when, having received the grace of Christ, he wants to extend it to others. It's true inside-out generosity!

When you give joyfully, your spirit reflects the generous spirit of God. It changes the way you see the world around you. And you begin to experience, in a deeper, more personal way, God's own joy and boundless love for all.

*Lord, help me to become a Scrooge... the end-of-the-story version, that is! Thank you for your gifts of grace lavished upon me. May I joyfully see them and spread them!*

# How Much Should I Give?

**"Jesus went over to the collection box in the Temple and sat and watched as the crowds dropped in their money. Many rich people put in large amounts. Then a poor widow came and dropped in two pennies. He called his disciples to him and said, 'I assure you, this poor woman has given more than all the others. For they gave a tiny part of their surplus, but she, poor as she is, has given everything she has.'"
Mark 12:41-44 (NLT)**

One of the most frequently asked questions about generosity that I get as a pastor is, "How much should I give?" Cult-like churches try to prescribe obligatory giving levels for everyone. Here's the truth: *You are the only person on earth who can decide what the right level of giving is for you.* It's not a genuine gift if it's given under compulsion.

While the amount of your giving is strictly personal, there are some universal principles in Scripture that are helpful as you determine your generosity strategy. Jesus pointed to the poor widow as a model in Mark 12:41-44. His point: God doesn't measure generosity by the size of the gift, but by the motivation. The widow in that story gave sacrificially out of her love for God and concern for the poor. I can't help but think of my own widowed mother, always so generous, despite her meager resources.

The generous believers in Macedonia are another great model of this kind of giving. Paul says of them, "For I can testify that they gave not only what they could afford, but much more. And they did it out of their own free will. They even begged us again and again for the gracious privilege of sharing in the gift for the Christians in Jerusalem." (2 Corinthians 8:3-4).

So God wants us to give generously, joyfully, and voluntarily (meaning, of our own will, not under any kind of pressure or compulsion).

The Apostle Paul also advises making a regular, prioritized habit of your giving: "On the first day of every week, set aside a sum proportionate to your income..." (1 Cor. 16:2). He's not saying you have to write your checks to charity and church only on Sundays. He's just saying, make it a habit. Don't wait until you win the lottery. The time to start making generosity a habit is *right now*. As Andy Stanley says, "When you make giving a priority, something happens inside you. It's like you loosen the grip of a value system whose motto is, 'Money is the key to life and happiness.'" When God blesses you, let your first action be a gesture that acknowledges where that blessing came from. For many people, the idea of generosity is stressful--because for them giving is always sporadic and a response to outside pressure. When it's a regular part of life, it's much less painful and much more joyful.

What about tithing? In the Hebrew Scriptures, all believers were required to give a tithe (ten percent of their income) to the poor and to God's work (See Leviticus 27:30). Although we are no longer under that law, many Christians choose to see the ten percent guideline as a great place to start. Why? It's easy to figure out, and it enables you to make substantial gifts.

But the ten percent guideline makes many Christians feel unnecessarily guilty if they don't keep it. Remember, the tithe is not a law that we must keep to earn merit in God's eyes. By the grace of God in Christ we already have God's unconditional love! I see the ten percent guideline as a useful tool for keeping my greed in check, and for keeping me challenged to give. I know many people who have a goal to reach ten percent giving, and then to grow their giving above and beyond that tithe.

The bottom line is, *the amount you give is between you and God.* Jesus says, "Then your Father, who sees what is done in secret, will reward you." (Matthew 6:4)

*Lord, please give me wisdom to know how to be joyfully and abundantly generous in my situation, and not worry about what others will think—or whether others even know.*

# Join the Discussion

**Social Media**
Share on our Facebook page what you are learning and the way you are noticing God's generous blessings to you!

**Sermons**
The sermons that tie into each week's material in this devotional can be downloaded or streamed for free at *tlc.org/richerlife*

**Small Group Discussion Material**
The questions on the following pages can be used for personal study, a couples' study, a family study with older children, or a small group study at work or church.

Each study includes these elements:
- **Discussion starter questions** designed to get people talking
- **Videos** you can watch on DVD or online at *tlc.org/richerlife*
- **Scripture reading and discussion questions** that follow
- **Homework** (suggestions on how to apply the principles we're learning)
- **Prayer** (I'll give you some suggestions for prayer; if this is a group study, you can also take prayer requests from group members, of course)

Please don't feel you need to cover all the questions. If you're leading a group, I suggest reading through the questions first and editing or adapting them as you see fit, just as I have edited and adapted them from a variety of sources.

Some questions in the weekly small group discussion guides are taken or adapted from:
- *Generosity: Responding to God's Radical Grace in Community* (New York: Redeemer Presbyterian, 2016)
- *Overflow: A Life Refreshed By Generosity* (GenerousChurch Inc, 2017)
- *Serendipity New Testament for Groups* (Grand Rapids: Zondervan, 1986)
- Andy Stanley, *How to Be Rich* (Grand Rapids: Zondervan, 2013)

# WEEK 1
# God's Lavish Grace

Big idea: God wants us to respond to his free gift of grace with the faith, gratitude, and generosity of a child.

**Discussion starter**
Begin with introductions. Share your name and where you grew up. What's one of the favorite gifts you've ever received, perhaps a memorable Christmas or birthday gift from your childhood? Why was it a favorite?

**In this series, we hope to get a better understanding of God's lavish gifts toward us—and the ways we can bring gifts to others!**

**Watch the video for week 1 on DVD or online at *tlc.org/ richerlife***

1. Why do you think so many people were inspired by this child's simple act of generosity?

2. Would an adult have been tempted to keep a baseball caught during a game rather than give it away? Why? Would you have kept it or shared it?

   **Now let's read Scripture about living in awareness of God's grace and having faith like a child!**

   **Have someone in your group read Luke 18:9-17 out loud.**

3. Jesus describes two men who went up to the temple to pray. To which of the two men in the story do you more readily relate? Or are there ways you can relate to both?

4. What is the Pharisee thankful for? What does this tell you about him?

5. Have you ever relied on good deeds to earn God's favor, like the Pharisee? How so?

6. Who are some of the "others" you're sometimes tempted to think of yourself as "better than", like the Pharisee did in this story?

7. How do you think Jesus wants us to be like little children? How does this relate to the parable of the two men?

**Have someone read Luke 15:11-32 out loud.**

8. This is a familiar story, but instead of focusing on the first son, look more closely at the second, in verses 30-32. Would you say the second son lived with a mindset of stinginess or of joyful generosity? What does the father say to him in verse 31? In what sense does God say the same thing to all believers?

   God wants us to live in full awareness of his riches that he has lavished on us. The reason the second son was so stingy toward the first is that he never understood that his father wanted him to enjoy his riches! It is so vital to "frame" our own life story within God's abundant generosity toward us!

9. How can an understanding of God's lavish generosity toward you radically change your motivation to do good deeds for others? Have you experienced this change in your own life?

**Closing Question**
What in this week's study has most challenged you, and why?

**Closing Prayer**
In your prayer time, confess any tendency to be self-reliant and proud instead of simply receiving God's grace. Confess how easily you can look down on "others". Ask God to help you grow in daily awareness of his blessings all around you!

# Cultivating Gratitude

**Discussion Starter**
What is something that happened to you this past week that you're thankful for?

Do you agree or disagree with this quote: "The problem with most of us is not that we're not rich; it's that we don't feel rich." –Andy Stanley

**Now watch the video for week 2 on DVD or online at *tlc.org/richerlife***

1.  What blessings does the narrator of the video describe that, in your opinion, many people don't even notice?

2.  What are some things that, when you take a moment to think about, you're very grateful for—yet you rarely actually give thanks for...

3.  How can practicing gratitude daily make you feel richer?

**Have someone read Philippians 4:6-19 out loud.**

4.  In verses 6-9, Paul talks about finding inner peace, serenity, and joy. How does he tell us to find these things? How do they relate to the video René showed?

5.  In verses 10-19, Paul thanks the Philippians for their generosity toward him. How is generosity an outflow of gratitude?

**Have someone read Luke 7:36-50 out loud.**

6.  What did the sinful woman understand about her sin and God's grace that Simon, the religious expert, did not understand?

7.  Let's talk about some specific things you're grateful for:

    What skills do you have that you are grateful for?

    What relationships do you have that you are grateful for?

    What opportunities have you had that you are grateful for?

    What are you grateful for about your faith—about what God has done for you in Christ?

## Homework
This week, keep a running inventory of specific ways God has been generous to you (You may have already begun the list in your daily devotions!). This could include spiritual, material, relational blessings—anything you think of. Plan to report back next week on some of the things you wrote.

## Closing Prayer
Have a time of group prayer centered on gratitude: If you feel comfortable, go around the room thanking God specifically for his love, and for other specific blessings—maybe some of the things you discussed in today's lesson.

# Generous Relationships

**Discussion Starter**
Have your group share 2 to 3 things from your "gratitude lists" you started last week:

**Now watch the video for week 3 on DVD or online at *tlc.org/ richerlife***

The short film in today's small group discussion starter is not a specifically Christian video; it's put out by a mental health organization. I point that out because it's important to understand, from a Christian perspective, that relational generosity is most effective when we are transformed from the inside-out by our knowledge of God's relational generosity toward us. We become more gracious to others when we see how God is gracious to us.

1.  What is your reaction to the short film René shows?

2.  What is the hardest thing for you when it comes to "relational generosity"?
    ___ Patience
    ___ Empathy
    ___ Giving others "space" when they're moody or upset
    ___ Not taking things personally
    ___ Not keeping score of the times I get the silent treatment
    ___ Other:

3.  In what ways do you think people are "relationally generous" with you? Do you tend to sulk, or get distracted, or forget chores, or get moody, or overwork, or put people down? (Or something else? Go ahead and confess it if you feel comfortable sharing!)

4.  What is the difference between being "relationally generous" and spoiling people, becoming co-dependent?
    **Have someone in your group read Luke 17:3-6.**

5.  How does Jesus' command to forgive differ from the way most people react to offenses? How is it different from the

ways we may have thought of forgiveness?

6. Can you relate to the disciples' response to this teaching? (See verse 5) Why do you think they said this?

7. In reply, Jesus talks about the power of faith. What do you think faith has to do with the command to forgive?

8. How does understanding God's grace to us radically transform the way we forgive others?

9. Have you ever forgiven someone who wronged you greatly? If you feel comfortable, share your story briefly with your group. What spiritual truths did you discover in your own journey toward forgiveness?

10. Is there someone you are struggling to forgive? You may not want to mention them by name if this is a sensitive situation, but share what you feel is appropriate with your group and ask for prayer—prayer for the faith to forgive as Christ commands.

**Homework**
Here's a fun homework assignment: This week, keep asking God to show you little ways you can be generous: in your relationships, with your resources, with your help, etc. Tell him that your eyes and ears are open to his direction. Then share with the group next week something you were able to do! Remember, you're not sharing to get the praise of others; you are sharing your stories to inspire others.

Also discuss ideas with your group for a "generosity project" you could all do together. Think of something you can do with your small group, family, or friends. One suggestion: You could all volunteer for a community service project!

**Closing Prayer**
Praise God for his endless forgiveness and radical kindness to us. Confess that our hearts can often be hard or uncaring toward one another. Ask that God would keep opening our eyes to his forgiveness and love, so that we would more readily forgive others.

# Holy Hospitality

The big idea: Jesus talked a lot about how hospitality with our homes and meals can be a blessing to others and reflects God's heart.

**Discussion Starter**

Last week our homework was to watch and listen for opportunities to be generous. Share about opportunities you had.

If you and your group did a generosity project together, debrief: How did it make you feel? Was there anything about it that made you uncomfortable? Did you feel closer to God afterwards? Were there any interesting experiences or insights you gained through your project?

Describe someone you know or have known who is exceptionally hospitable. What did they do habitually that makes you think of them as hospitable?

**Now watch the video for week 4 on DVD or online at *tlc.org/ richerlife***

1.  How do you feel about this child's decision to distribute "blessing bags"?

2.  Does anything about this idea make you uncomfortable?

    **Have someone in your group read Luke 14:12-24**

3.  If you extended hospitality to the "poor, crippled, lame, and blind" in your community, who would they be? How could you show hospitality to them?

4.  What do you think is Jesus' point in the parable?

    **One of Mother Teresa's favorite texts in the Bible, which she often quoted to support her ministry to the poor, is Matthew 25:31-46. Have someone in your group read it aloud.**

5. List the six actions the King commends in verses 35-36:

6. Besides those mentioned here, who else might be "the least of these"?

7. Have you ever been in one of these six categories and had someone reach out to you? What happened?

8. In these six areas, where do you find yourself serving most naturally? In which areas do you have the most difficulty?

9. Have you ever found it rewarding to be involved in ministry to people in these categories? What did you do? How did it impact you? (Share with the group so that they might be inspired to join you!)

**Homework**
If you have not had a chance to do a "generosity project" yet with your group, discuss some ideas. Perhaps you can contribute to the "Project Pajamas" goal, or to another project. Maybe you have an elderly neighbor who could use help. Maybe you could all volunteer at the food bank or People's Pantry. Our regular ministries could also use help, like our children's ministry and the ushers and communion servers.

**Closing Prayer**
Praise God for inviting us to his lavish kingdom feast! Thank him that we do not have to earn our way in, but that Jesus already did that for us all! Confess that sometimes we are not free with our hospitality or generosity. Ask for a deeper understanding of the gospel message, of God's hospitality to us. Ask that this would cause us to show no-strings-attached grace to others, especially those on the margins of society.

# My Source of Security

The big idea: There is a link between generous living and knowing where my true security really lies: The grace of God!

**Discussion Starter**
If you had to give up one "luxury" in your home, what would be the first to go? What would be the last to go? Coffee maker? TV? Computer? Wifi? DVR? Washer/dryer? Indoor toilet? Comfortable bed? Other?

How is this study affecting you so far? Did you take a step of faith in generosity this past week? If you feel comfortable, share your story with the group. Shared stories inspire and encourage!

**Now open your Bibles to Acts 20:32-35 and watch the video for week 5 on DVD or online at *tlc.org/richerlife***
(Thanks to Redeemer Presbyterian Church NYC for the video resource)

As you watch, listen for:
- The link between grace and generosity
- The rich meaning of the word "blessed"
- The best motivation for generosity

1. What stood out to you most from Keller's message?

2. What link does he draw between the gospel and our generosity?

3. How did this video impact your thinking about living generously?

4. In what ways have you experienced that it really is "more blessed to give than to receive"?

**Have someone read Luke 18:18-30 out loud.**

5. The rich young ruler claimed he had faithfully kept all

the commandments since his youth. Why then was it so difficult for him to follow Jesus' command in verse 22?

6. Is Jesus' command to sell everything and give it all to the poor required of everyone? Why or why not? (This might spark some lively discussion! Debate respectfully!)

**Verses About the Truly Rich Life**
The Bible talks a lot about what a truly rich life is, and how important it is to keep wealth and success in perspective. From the list below, choose a verse that is especially meaningful to you. Then take turns sharing which verse you chose and why.

Do not wear yourself out to get rich; do not trust your own cleverness. Cast but a glance at riches, and they are gone, for they will surely sprout wings and fly off to the sky like an eagle. Proverbs 23:4-5

Listen, my dear brothers and sisters: Has not God chosen those who are poor in the eyes of the world to be rich in faith and to inherit the kingdom he promised those who love him? James 2:5

Command those who are rich in this present world not to be arrogant nor to put their hope in wealth, which is so uncertain, but to put their hope in God, who richly provides us with everything for our enjoyment. 1 Timothy 6:17

Moreover, when God gives someone wealth and possessions, and the ability to enjoy them, to accept their lot and be happy in their toil—this is a gift of God. Ecclesiastes 5:19

(Jesus said) "No one can serve two masters. Either you will hate the one and love the other, or you will be devoted to the one and despise the other. You cannot serve both God and money." Luke 16:13

I know what it is to be in need, and I know what it is to have plenty. I have learned the secret of being content in any and every situation, whether well fed or hungry, whether living in plenty or in want. I can do all things through him who gives me strength. Philippians 4:12-13

Jesus said, "I tell you the truth, anyone who gives a cup of water in my name because you belong to Christ will certainly not lose his reward." Mark 9:41

"The Lord Jesus himself said, 'It is more blessed to give than to receive.'" Acts 20:35b

## Homework
If you have not done a generosity project together with your group yet, decide tonight what you will do.

## Closing Prayer
Pray that you will each experience God's generosity to you—and have a chance to treat others generously—in exciting ways this week. Pray for open eyes to blessings and opportunities to bless others!

# WEEK 6

# My Resources
# & God's Power

The big idea: When I risk involvement, Jesus multiplies my resources into generous ministry to others!

**Discussion starter**
How is this study affecting you so far?

Would you say you frame your life story as one of abundance or scarcity? How does this impact your "giving identity"?

**Now watch the video for week 6 on DVD or online at
*tlc.org/richerlife***
(Thanks to GenerousChurch for the video resource)

1.  What stood out to you most from Evelyn's story?

2.  What words would you use to describe Evelyn's facial expressions?

3.  She's a great example of what's been called "whole-life generosity": Rooted in God's grace, and thus giving to others joyfully. Quickly list 2-3 ways, besides giving money, that we can be generous:

    **When you think about generosity, you might think you have little to give. I love Peter's statement to the beggar in Acts 3:6, "Silver and gold have I none, but what I *have* I give to you..." Let's look at a story that illustrates this. Have someone read the famous story in Luke 9:10-17 out loud.**

4.  What tones of voice do you hear in verse 11 and verse 12? How would you describe the differences in how Jesus looks at the crowd and how the disciples see the crowd? How do you account for this difference?

5.  How would you feel as a disciple after you had seen the

crowd fed and you'd gathered all the leftovers? What do you think Jesus is trying to teach his disciples here? (Remember, he is training them for the worldwide ministry we see them having in the Book of Acts, where they have very little in the way of resources but are able to have global impact)

6.  How have you seen Jesus stretch your resources far beyond what you'd imagined? If you feel comfortable, share a story that demonstrates this from your own life.

7.  As you think back over what we've covered in the last 6 weeks about a richer life, what is one message God seems to be continually bringing back to you?

**Closing Prayer**
We have learned that God is your provider. He can meet your needs abundantly, no matter how scarce your resources. Trusting in his care defeats fear. So today ask God to help you put your ultimate trust in him and not in any worldly resources. Ask him to help you take more "generosity risks", both to draw you closer to him and to spread the kingdom of God.

# WEEK 7
# Inside-Out Generosity

The big idea: When I have been transformed by God's generosity toward me, I will be generous toward others. And when I am generous, I will be blessed.

**Discussion Starters**
Do you tend to be a risk-taker or a more safety-minded person? Give examples.

Did you have opportunities to show generosity in some way (in relationships, in service to others, in hospitality, in giving resources) this past week? If you feel comfortable, share an experience with the group (remember, shared stories inspire others!). How did you grow or learn through this experience?

**Now watch the video for week 7 on DVD or online at** *tlc.org/richerlife*
(Thanks to GenerousChurch for today's video of Francis Chan)

1. What stood out to you most from Francis Chan's comments? Do you agree or disagree?

2. Have you seen anyone drawn to faith because of a church's generosity?

3. Do you agree with the statement: "You can give without loving, but you can't love without giving"?

   **Have someone in your group read Luke 19:1-23 out loud.**

4. In Luke 18, Jesus tells the rich young ruler to sell everything he owns and give it to the poor, and that man goes away sad. Here, a few verses later, Zacchaeus offers to give away half of what he owns, and Jesus is delighted. Why does he ask for 100% from one and 50% from another? What's the lesson you can draw from this? (Hint: It's not about the amount, it's about the _____ )

5. In the devotions, René writes about a study on "luck". To summarize: The research shows that, over time, people who thought of themselves as "lucky" risked more, took more chances, and said "yes" to more opportunities. Those who labeled themselves "unlucky" were very conservative, never took risks, and stayed within their comfort zones. Thus, the "lucky" were there to seize great opportunities when they came along. How does this remind you of the parable of the talents in Luke 19?

6. In this and other parables, does Jesus seem to advocate for more adventurous investment for the kingdom or for more safety?

7. How have you seen God bless your efforts when you have put your "talents" into circulation, even when you have been a little afraid to do so? If you feel comfortable, share a story that might inspire others in your group.

## Wrapping Up Our Series
As you look back over the seven weeks of this study, what big idea does God seem to be teaching you?

## Generosity Verses
Here are some verses about the concepts we've covered in this study. From the list below, choose a verse that is especially meaningful to you. Then take turns sharing which verse you chose and why.

Jesus said, "I tell you the truth, anyone who gives a cup of water in my name because you belong to Christ will certainly not lose his reward." Mark 9:41

The Lord Jesus himself said, "It is more blessed to give than to receive." Acts 20:35b

Do not forget to show hospitality to strangers, for by so doing some people have shown hospitality to angels without knowing it. Hebrews 13:2

Be kind and compassionate to one another, forgiving each other, just as in Christ God forgave you. Ephesians 4:32

And let us consider how we may spur one another on to love and good deeds. Hebrews 10:24

Suppose a brother or a sister is without clothes and daily food. If one of you says to them, "Go in peace; keep warm and well fed," but does nothing about their physical needs, what good is it? James 2:15-16

I have learned the secret of being content in any and every situation, whether well fed or hungry, whether living in plenty or in want. I can do all things through him who gives me strength. Philippians 4:12b-13

And God is able to bless you abundantly, so that in all things at all times, having all that you need, you will abound in every good work. 2 Corinthians 9:8

You will be enriched in every way so that you can be generous on every occasion, and through us your generosity will result in thanksgiving to God. 2 Corinthians 9:11

Command those who are rich in this present world not to be arrogant nor to put their hope in wealth, which is so uncertain, but to put their hope in God, who richly provides us with everything for our enjoyment. 1 Timothy 6:17

Moreover, when God gives someone wealth and possessions, and the ability to enjoy them, to accept their lot and be happy in their toil—this is a gift of God. Ecclesiastes 5:19

## Closing Prayer

As this study comes to a close, pray together that God will help you each continue to grow in a "generosity mindset" as we see the abundance of blessings God pours on us. Please pray that our church will continue to wisely "invest our talents". Ask God to help you continue to trust in him as your perfect provider.

# Resources

Although I didn't footnote each citation or contribution, I want to acknowledge that many of the illustrations and ideas in this book are from these great resources on generosity:

John Alexander, *Your Money or Your Life* (San Francisco: Harper & Row, 1986)

Ken Blanchard and S. Truett Cathy, *The Generosity Factor: Discover the Joy of Giving Your Time, Talent, and Treasure* (Grand Rapids: Zondervan, 2010)

John Cortines and Gregory Baumer, *God and Money: How We Discovered True Riches at Harvard Business School* (Carson: Rose, 2016)

Andrew Field, *Generosity: How God's Radical Grace Changes Our Perspective on Money and Possessions* (New York: Redeemer Presbyterian, 2016)

Jennifer Iacovelli, *Simple Giving: Easy Ways to Give Every Day* (New York: Jeremy P. Tarcher/Penguin, 2015)

Gordon MacDonald, *Generosity: Moving Toward Life That Is Truly Life* (Generous Church, 2014)

*On Managing Yourself* (Boston: Harvard Business Review Press, 2010)

*Overflow: A Life Refreshed By Generosity* (Generous Church, 2017)

Rick Rusaw and Brian Mavis, *The Neighboring Church* (Nashville: Thomas Nelson, 2016)

Robert Morris, *The Blessed Life* (Grand Rapids: Bethany House, 2004)

Todd Sinelli, *True Riches* (Santa Cruz: Lit Torch, 2001)

Andy Stanley, *How to Be Rich* (Grand Rapids: Zondervan, 2013)

John Stott, *The Grace of Giving* (Hendrickson, 2012)

Laura Sumner Truax and Amalya Campbell, *Love Let Go: Radical Generosity for the Real World* (Grand Rapids: Eerdmans, 2017)

John Thornton, *Jesus' Terrible Financial Advice* (Chicago: Moody, 2017)

Ben Witherington, *Jesus and Money* (Grand Rapids: Baker, 2010)

# SMALL GROUP PRAYER REQUESTS

_____

_____

_____

_____

_____

_____

_____

_____

_____

_____

_____

_____

_____

_____

_____

_____

_____

_____

# SMALL GROUP PRAYER REQUESTS

_____

_____

_____

_____

_____

_____

_____

_____

_____

_____

_____

_____

_____

_____

_____

_____

# GRATITUDE JOURNAL
**(continued from page 7)**

Ron

My daughters

Grandchilden

Family

Church

Dear

Nature, etc.

Success Super

Content

God's

on

# GRATITUDE JOURNAL

# GRATITUDE JOURNAL

---

# Other Books and Small Group Studies by René Schlaepfer

Thrill Ride
The Hope Experience
Grace Immersion
God Is
Jesus Journey
The Seven
Acts Odyssey

For more free resources related to "Richer Life"
including sermons and videos, visit **tlc.org/richerlife**